Angry Little Men:
Hypermasculinity, Academic Disconnect,
and
Mentoring African American Males

Kevin Todd Porter

Chicago, Illinois

Front cover illustration by Damon Stanford

First Edition, First Printing

Printed in the United States of America

ISBN #: 1-913543-81-0
ISBN #: 9-781934-155-81-3

This book is dedicated to the memory of my two childhood best friends, Robert Ford, Jr. and Bronson Drew, taken away too soon.

I also dedicate this book to my family and friends who have encouraged and inspired me throughout the years.

Contents

Introduction: A Look Inside v

1. Why Are African American Boys So Angry? 1

2. Academic Self-Concept 5

3. Academic Self-Concept of African American

   Males 23

4. Hypermasculine Identity Development 47

5. School Engagement 59

6. Investigation of Hypermasculinity and School

   Engagement 67

7. Angry Little Men 91

Appendix A: Tables from Research 106

Appendix B: School District Demographics 110

Bibliography 111

Introduction: A Look Inside

Step into any classroom in inner-city America, and there's going to be a mix of students: some who want to learn and some who are disengaged—all too often taking attention from students who want to reach academic goals. From the outside looking in, it might appear that an overwhelmingly large percentage of African American at-risk males come off as little angry men. At-risk males bring a totally different mindset to the classroom. That's because education is way down on a list of their priorities that might include drugs, gangs, chasing girls, or just trying to survive a disruptive home life. For many, their worlds are more connected to images found in hip-hop or a thug life culture that doesn't easily accept or promote African American males who embrace making academia a priority. Sure, they realize that school is important. But too often maintaining a street image trumps education— despite evidence of a disproportionate amount of academic failures in their communities and the knowledge that education can offer a brighter future.

This book is aimed at offering insight for new and experienced teachers and mentors who have the desire and calling to work with kids, but find it difficult to reach a certain group of young males—in particular, African American males. It offers a view that few authors have examined called hypermasculine identity—or male bravado—as a significant contributor to disengagement. A lot of books and studies suggest that negative outcomes faced by at-risk youth are associated with race and poverty, but very few investigate a developmental trajectory as to why African American males suffer dramatically in school, leading to bleak future employment opportunities or often inclusion in the criminal justice system. Even fewer studies and books focus on this trajectory as it relates to the notion of hypermasculine identity among African American male adolescents.

What does hypermasculinity mean? A number of details will help us bring this term to life:

- Excessiveness—even minor situations get blown out of proportion;
- Disconnectedness—nonchalance tends to be the response to matters that adults at school treat as important, such as grades and homework;
- Physical strength—very interested in displays of prowess and aggression, and in defending the quality of physical strength;
- Undisciplined approach to personal attitudes, speech, behavior, and outlook;
- Callous attitude toward females of most ages (i.e., misogyny);
- Relationships devoid of success;
- Disowning responsibility for personal shortcomings.

Taken together, we can visualize the makeup of hypermasculine African American youth as we encounter them inside and outside the classroom.

My pursuit of finding an answer to why so many at-risk males underachieve and why many well-intentioned educators, mentors, and parents have basically given up, didn't

Introduction

exactly start out as my initial goal. In fact, the first time I attempted to participate in a mentoring program I was a recent college graduate with an engineering degree, who participated in a fraternity-associated community service project just outside of Chicago. At the time, I had the "I got mine, you get yours" attitude—but I was there to be an example. After months of encouraging good grades, discouraging fighting, taking teenage males on field trips and even observing them consider college as an option, their initial demeanor of apathy and coldness was replaced with loosening up and embracing change. But I'll never forget how one particular kid—whom I thought was among the ones who showed the most promise—changed my entire concept and belief that kids just need to spend time with good role models who care. One day as this teenager left our classroom, I watched him transform at the sight of his friends as he headed down the hall to join them. Suddenly his walk, demeanor, and dialogue were totally different from just a few minutes earlier when he was with our group. That's when a light turned on for me as to why they were "good boys" in our presence who emerged as "little angry men" as soon as our mentoring sessions ended. At-risk boys are constantly trying to fit in and maintain their street image during school and outside of school. They adopt a posture and speech of hypermasculinity. It's a path I walked myself—but chose to leave behind and forget—because I was among the lucky ones who managed to downplay my academic achievements in high school except for sports. My closest friends didn't find out I ranked second in my class until graduation. Years later, I realized how important it was for me to do what I call "C.O.D.E. switch," if I was going to be successful after high school. For me, the idea of playing down academics around my friends started my freshman year in high school on a bus ride home on report card day. That's when I complained about getting a C in gym class and they bragged about higher grades in that class. Then their moods changed as soon as they saw that the rest of my grades were A's. They weighed in hard with insults and made me feel like an outcast because the rest of their report cards ranged from C's to F's. For a moment I almost felt bad about succeeding in school. Then I realized that academics were important to achieve my goals. It's a fine line, though, because as an African American male growing up in an at-risk environment, maintaining my friendships was just as important. I worked hard at keeping both worlds separate from my friends.

The piercing reality is that the environment I grew up in violently took away many young men who embraced this hypermasculine identity—including my two closest friends who teased me about getting good grades on that bus ride home. One of them, who never backed down from a fight, was killed at age 19 just two years after we graduated. My other closest friend was shot in the head when he was 25 years old. He was left blind, and passed away several years later. I recall how important we thought being tough was. Not backing down from anyone was our claim to manhood. But looking back years later, I realized that if not for that mindset, they might be here today.

My first mentoring experience forced me to reflect. It also led to mentoring for the next 20 years in Texas while working in roles that ranged from being an engineer and then an entrepreneur,

Introduction

teaching math and science in an urban at-risk community in Dallas and obtaining an M.S. in psychological sciences. I wanted to study data and evaluate developmental issues of at-risk students—and collect my own data. One factor that I examined was an indicator called "self-concept" used by psychologists to determine what makes kids feel positive about themselves. It led me to question why or how one's belief about their academic self did not correlate with academic performance on tests. I couldn't understand why two students with the same level of academic belief often had such different levels of performance. That's when I realized that most of the at-risk males I have mentored are very confident about their academic ability. Unfortunately, they have just chosen not to stretch their minds. The great challenge has been investing enough positive time so that at-risk males trust the direction necessary to becoming successful in school. From a hypermasculine perspective, school performance is not generally the only area that gives them the greatest satisfaction. Respect from others means more. Most at-risk males have embraced the hip-hop image of dressing the part, looking the part, and disregarding the intellectual aspect of continuous learning in school.

Hypermasculinity has been the protective mechanism that most at-risk males hide behind so that no one bothers them, encourages them to engage, or places high expectations on them. However, without the proper understanding of why someone would purposely become disengaged in school it is difficult to change the behavior. When we become aware of some of the developmental challenges of at-risk males then we become better equipped to address changes we want to see as parents, teachers, or mentors.

My goal in writing this book is to offer a different perspective about why some at-risk kids are going to make it through the system and become excellent citizens in our great country, while a large part of the African American at-risk male population will continue to struggle beyond school or drop out. It often boils down to a lack of investment of one-on-one time from a trusting relationship—because gaining trust takes time. It's even more difficult for educators forced to compete with what seems like overwhelming odds, including crowded classrooms that include students dealing with street codes and credibility issues associated with maintaining reputations.

You just can't underestimate the power of hypermasculinity and its impact on education. I believe helping students begins with them finding success in small chunks, especially for at-risk students, who have failed to discover their academic strengths.

Chapter 1: Why Are African American Boys So Angry?

If there are at-risk boys, there must be at-risk parents and families. If parents and families are at risk, then there are at-risk schools that operate in at-risk communities. If our communities are at risk, then cities are at risk. If our cities are at risk, then states are at risk. If states are at risk, then America is at risk. So the question is: Why are there so many boys at risk in America?

How do you reach a young man, an angry little man, with so much talent and so much of the world for him to conquer—whose perception seems so squelched of the strategies and resources readily available for him to tap? His bravado is so intense that he respects no one, yet he wants to be respected by everyone. His inability to communicate his feelings usually results in an angry episode that shows disrespect for himself and others. As a young man, he has not mastered the first lesson he wants others to abide by: to get respect, you must show respect. Anger has caused him to lose control of his emotions, even in the battle of friendly competition. Over time the results of his anger will be disastrous if he doesn't gain control of it.

Why do African American boys get so upset? Boys who exhibit toughness and anger are also full of play, full of dreams, but they don't know how they will achieve those dreams, and they refuse to obey authority or heed the wisdom of their elders. Lacking vision, understanding, and discretion, they become angry little men. I use this term not in a demeaning way, but with concern because I understand that boys wear what I call a "mask of

Angry Little Men: Hypermasculinity, Academic Disconnect, and Mentoring African American Males

Hypermasculinity" for the purpose of protection from authority and a reaction against anything that challenges their power.

The anger of at-risk African American males can be seen in their behaviors, demeanor, music choices, and rebellious style. Seldom do they look like happy adolescents. They have a chip on the shoulder that demands the respect they think they deserve as "men." In fact, their anger is a sign of insecurity and a lack of knowledge regarding the responsibilities of a true man of conviction and integrity. The mask of Hypermasculinity and anger protects their dreams, fears, and who they want to become. They think they must wear this mask to pass as men, but they will soon realize that the mask does not equal manhood and that in fact, they are going the wrong way.

What's wrong with our angry little men and what do we do in response? When and where does this anger most often occur? How and when do we confront this anger? How do we help our angry little men grow up to become good, loving men?

This writing began as a personal quest to reveal the hopes and dreams of young African American boys whose true identities lay hidden behind a mask of hypermasculinity. African American boys are also attempting to discover their own hearts and souls, but the mask has created a blind spot. It distances males from academic success, opportunities in the mainstream, healthy relationships with females and each other, and positive future outcomes. The mask distances young males from awareness of themselves.

I wrote this book to explain how a young man's bravado, his hypermasculine mask, is related to his engagement or success in the classroom. Other important questions this book asks include:

Chapter 1: Why Are African American Boys So Angry?

- Why do at-risk males use bravado (Hypermasculinity) in the classroom and beyond?
- How does bravado (Hypermasculinity) help at-risk males navigate the unchartered waters of life?

This book focuses on three parts to understanding at-risk males: addressing the view on Academic Self-Concept, a look at Male Bravado (Hypermasculity), and School Engagement. I explore literature from various periods in history and bring the material to today's world of hip-hop and the evolution of male identity in the form of Hypermasculinity theory. The findings in this book provide a basis for at-risk males developmental theory for academic disconnect and how this cycle impacts the various mentoring programs geared toward making a difference in their lives. We will investigate the mindset and life experiences that play a critical role in identity formation, academic performance, and future outcomes for at-risk boys. We will conclude with a discussion of the C.O.D.E. switch African American males will need to master to become positive contributors to society, and some of the ways (e.g., mentoring) we can help them succeed at home, in the classroom, and in life.

This book includes actual research collected for my master's thesis, "The Developmental Investigation of Hypermasculinity and School Disengagement." The research provides empirical support for Hypermasculinity being prevalent in at-risk communities. I explored several questions related to the Hypermasculinity of boys in various settings, including single-parent homes and school (i.e., academic disengagement). In addition, I examined peer pressure, the presence (or lack thereof) of the father, and the day-to-day life "hassles," all of which affect the academic disconnect of at-risk boys.

Hypermasculinity in African American males is projected to the world as a negative and angry demeanor, and this has led to harmful stereotypes and discriminatory practices in the classroom and among mainstream society. *Little Angry Men: Hypermasculinity, Academic Disconnect, and Mentoring African American Males* takes an honest look at Hypermasculinity and helps the unaware observer, parent, teacher, or mentor understand the survival function of the mask behind which these young men hide their fears in order to gain respect.

I hope this book guides those individuals who have a desire to make a positive impact, to be more effective with the boys they are mentoring, teaching, and parenting.

Every child is at-risk if we don't take the time to understand them.

Chapter 2: Academic Self-Concept

Understanding one's ability is critical to setting and reaching one's goal. We learn various things about academic success based on students' beliefs about their academic ability. One common indicator used by psychologists and researchers is the term Academic Self-Concept. Academic self-concept is an important indicator of academic success for most kids. The low academic performance of African American males, as well as their high dropout rate and low college attendance, have been widely researched and reported. Yet we know little about how their academic self-concept is formed and how it correlates with academic performance. In my opinion, this is a glaring omission in the literature.

This chapter lays the foundation for Chapter 3, which delves deeply into the academic self-concept of African American males. In this chapter, I will:

- Define self-concept and the emerging self;
- Describe some beliefs and multidimensional theories of self-concept;
- Summarize the existing literature on academic self-concept;
- Explain how academic self-concept correlates with objective standards of achievement (i.e., grades and standardized tests);
- Probe differences between the academic self-concept of African American and Anglo male students.

5

Angry Little Men: Hypermasculinity, Academic Disconnect, and Mentoring African American Males

The academic self-concept of Anglo males is the benchmark against which all other groups are measured. The literature (Marsh 1987; Shavelson et al. 1976) suggests that at least for Anglo middle-class students, academic self-concept is a reliable indicator of academic achievement. We will determine if this assumption holds true for the many African American males who are currently struggling academically. Finally, this chapter introduces life experiences of African American males and several theoretical models that seek to explain unique aspects of self-concept in stigmatized groups, such as minorities, that may serve as an explanation for the discrepancies that exist in previous research. These discrepancies provide some explanation about how African American males may cope with their issues associated with prejudice, discrimination, and being a minority male.

The Theory of Self-Concept

Theories of self and self-worth have been investigated by psychologists (Cooley 1902; James 1892; Mead 1934) since at least the late 1800s. Cooley (1902) and Mead (1934) believed that feelings about the self were shaped mostly by the appraisals of other people. James (1892) theorized that the self is developed through social interactions and personal accomplishments. He believed that we are all actors with multiple selves and that there are as many social selves as there are mental images of the self. These multiple images help shape our most important and valuable experiences. How we perceive our experiences and accomplishments creates self-worth (or the lack thereof). For example, if one sees science as a subject that is unimportant, then his failure or lack of competency in science will not affect his self-worth. Recent psychologists (Ross 1992) have described self-concept as the representation of how one thinks and feels about self—in other words, self-perception.

Overall, the literature suggests that a positive self-concept will lead to constructive, socially desirable behaviors; conversely, a distorted self-concept will lead to socially deviant behaviors (Scheirer & Kraut 1979).

The Emerging Self

How the self emerges is going to be a very critical factor when we examine the many distractions and obstacles associated with at-risk communities. Cooley (1902) said we all have what he called a "looking-glass self." He theorized that the self is inseparable from social life and is thus shaped by relationships with others. From early childhood, our concept of self develops from seeing how others respond to us. We adopt or mimic the traits of those closest to us.

Mead's (1934) investigations led to an amplified version of Cooley's looking-glass self. Mead suggested that individuals experience themselves as reflections of others in their same social group. For example, an individual judges his worthiness or social status by comparing himself with others in his income bracket, neighborhood, ethnic group, etc. Mead's looking-glass self not only reflects significant others, as Cooley suggested, but one's entire socio-cultural environment.

Angry Little Men: Hypermasculinity, Academic Disconnect, and Mentoring African American Males

Mead, Cooley, and James laid the foundation for the study of self, but their theories stopped short of explaining how self-awareness or self-perception develops during childhood. Susan Harter (1986) offers a developmental perspective of the self and how it evolves.

Harter says that as a child's cognitive abilities develop, so does self-awareness. The construction of the self during childhood embraces an understanding of "I" and "Me," where "I" is the knower and "Me" represents an aggregate of things objectively known. As children begin to distinguish "I" from "Me," they begin to form a more objective self-concept. This objective self-concept allows the child to realize that now he can assume the perspective of others, allowing the theory of self to change how the child views self. At this stage the child begins to learn from others what they see as true or believed about themselves or others. This progression of knowledge illustrates how the judgments of significant others (telling the child that he is bad, cute, smart, etc.) affect self-concept. Harter says that this ability to consider the viewpoint of others has important implications for the development of self-awareness.

As children grow and begin to think about their world and how it impacts the lives of others, this also affects the development of self. Harter (1986) illustrates how these changing structures, based on the Piagetian perspective, may affect the theory of self.

Piaget was very important in discovering and understanding the behavior of children as he described their behavior through various developmental stages. In Piagetian theory, there are four critical periods of development from infancy to adulthood:

sensorimotor, pre-operational, concrete operational, and formal operational. Harter says that the pre-operational, concrete operational, and formal operational periods are critical to the development of self-awareness and awareness of others. During the pre-operational period (two to six years of age), a child has a proliferation of categories that he can use to define the self. For example, during the preschool years, the child may describe himself as smart, big, or good. These highly generalizable terms are used because the child has not yet acquired the ability to objectively view his behavior; therefore, the all-or-none relationships are used during this period. The pre-operational child does not yet possess the role-taking skills necessary to cognitively construct Cooley's looking-glass self. It is during the next stage, the concrete operational period, that the emergence of logical thinking produces qualitative changes in the nature of the child's self-theory.

As the child transitions from the pre-operational period to the concrete period (7 to 11 years of age), he changes cognitively: he learns how to read, work with numbers, form relationships, judge others, and distinguish right from wrong. Upon entering the concrete operational period, there is the emergence of logical thinking which produces qualitative changes in the nature of the child's self-theory. It is in this stage that the child has the ability to hierarchically classify and logically organize concrete events, objects, and people. Harter (1986) says that during this stage, the child is expected to judge certain traits of the self, specifically his observable concrete characteristics. This verification is made through the child's own view of self as well as from the direct and indirect feedback of others. For example, the child determines that the observable concrete characteristic of being "likable" can be attributed to the number of friends he has or how well he gets along with his friends. Additional cognitive characteristics at this stage provide the child with the ability to form some hierarchical organization; for example, "I'm smart (higher order trait) because I'm good at reading, spelling, and math (lower order behavioral characteristics)." The concrete operational child, therefore, has attributive and categorical knowledge that apply to the self which will assist the child as he approaches the formal operational stage.

As the child enters the formal operational stage (12 to 17 years of age), he begins to formulate and test hypotheses about himself and his environment. During this stage the child begins transitioning from dependence on adults and parents to independence, embracing his own opinions about self rather than his parents'. The child becomes more tuned in to his peers, wanting to be accepted by them rather than that which has been prescribed by parents. The adolescent is ready to test his abilities, personality, and view of self with the rest of the world, and this is done through role playing. The adolescent now realizes that he can act intelligently, pretend to be happy, be aggressive when necessary, and even act like an adult. Role playing enables the child to see that he is now an integral part of a larger social group (e.g., middle class, Democrats, Texans, African Americans).

The adolescent now realizes that he is a member of society. Later he will begin to think logically, which includes the ability to hierarchically classify and logically organize concrete events, objects, and people. These stages lay the foundation for the all-

Chapter 2: Academic Self-Concept

important, multidimensional self-concept as suggested by theorists such as Marsh (1990), Shavelson and Bolus (1982), and Bryne (1986).

Conversely, a child's attempt to organize, summarize, or explain his behavior results in the formation of cognitive structures about the self. Thus, as he cognitively develops, he gains self-awareness, and as self-awareness grows, so does cognition. It is believed that those with a well-defined understanding of traits within the self can more readily process self-related information, retrieve behavioral evidence, and predict future behavior (Harter 1986). As the understanding of self-concept continues and its functionality analyzed, the literature suggests that the structure of self-concept becomes multidimensional. Therefore, we are left with two important questions:

- What are the dimensions of self-concept?
- Can self-concept predict future outcomes, especially academic achievement?

Multidimensionality of Self-Concept and Hierarchical Structure

The long history of psychological research regarding self-concept has been plagued by simplistic theoretical models, poor instrumentation, and methodological shortcomings that limit its utility (Marsh 1991). At best, one-dimensional structures of self-concept were yielded.

Self-concept modeling has been greatly enhanced and influenced by the ideas of Shavelson et al. (1976). They proposed that self-concept is a multifaceted, hierarchical construct that becomes increasingly articulated with age. Shavelson found that infants tend not to differentiate themselves from their environment, but as they mature and learn from their experiences, differentiation of self from environment begins. With young children, the self-concepts are global, undifferentiated, and situation-specific (e.g., "I'm liked, therefore I'm smart"). As children begin to build concepts, as represented by the words "I" and "Me," they also begin to build concepts for categorizing events and situations. With increasing age and experience, self-concept becomes increasingly differentiated. Shavelson suggests that an individual's experiences, however diverse, collect the data by which he perceives himself. To reduce the complexity of these experiences, a person recodes them into simpler forms, or categories. According to Shavelson, the particular category systems adopted by an individual are to some extent a reflection of his particular culture or subculture. The multidimensional, hierarchical category system of Anglo middle-class students appears to include such areas as school, social acceptance, physical attractiveness, and academic ability.

Marsh (1987) attempted to demonstrate that facets of self-concept range from an individual's experiences at the base of the hierarchy to general self-concept at the apex. He divided general self-concept into two components for students: academic self-concept and non-academic self-concept. Academic self-concept may be divided into areas of subject matter which in turn can be further divided. Nonacademic self-concept may be divided into social and physical self-concept and then divided into more specific facets in a manner similar to academic self-concept. (Although nonacademic self-concept plays an integral role in the development of self, this chapter will focus on academic self-concept and its impact on the academic achievements of students, specifically African American males.)

Marsh used an instrument called the Self-Description Questionnaire (SDQ) to determine the validity of his model. The SDQ results provided strong support for Shavelson's model and the multidimensionality of self-concept. The findings illustrated that while general self-concept resides at the apex of the hierarchy, the underlying substructure is comprised of many aspects of self, each somewhat autonomous from the other but assimilated together at each supraordinated level. For example, math performance contributes to a child's math self-concept which in turn is a part of the broader academic self-concept—a component of general self-concept. This provides substantial data for multidimensional models of self-concept and shows how developmental changes in cognition enable the child to organize information about the world in more complex ways, thus creating an increasingly sophisticated view of self (Harter 1986; Marsh 1990; Marsh 1991; Marsh & Shavelson 1985).

It's important to note that these studies, though groundbreaking, were based on observations of middle-class Anglo students, which brings into question their validity for children of other income classes, cultures, and racial groups.

Academic Self-Concept and Achievement in Anglo Students

Since academic self-concept seems to be an important indicator to school success, how likely does it predict success on academic achievement? Standard models describing the relationship between self-concept and academic achievement are not universally applicable to all groups. However, in this section we will review the literature on Anglo students to see if the models might be useful for African American male students. We will consider whether academic self-concept contributes to academic achievement, and we will review the analyses of Shavelson et al. (1976) and other researchers. Most importantly, we will begin to look at the relationship of academic self-concept to socioeconomic status and race, and academic self-concept to academic achievement.

Does academic self-concept contribute or predict academic achievement? What interests most researchers is how improvement of self-concept (how you feel about who you are) may lead to improvements in other areas such as academic achievement (Calsyn and Kenny 1977). Hansford and Hattie (1982) and Shavelson and Bolus (1982) found positive correlations between academic self-concept and academic achievement. Hansford and Hattie concluded that there is a relatively strong relationship between self and measures of academic performance/achievement for most students. Similar findings by Shavelson and Bolus (1982), conclude that the relation between self-concept and indices of achievement such as grades and test scores. As a result, many educators have concluded that if academic self-concept increases, then so does academic performance. Further review of the empirical data supporting the hierarchical structure and strong correlation of academic achievement with self-concept will illustrate the importance placed on this success indicator.

According to several studies (Byrne 1986; Hansford & Hattie 1982; Marsh et al. 1983; Shavelson & Bolus 1982, self-concept is hierarchical in structure, starting with perceptions of behavior at the base, to inferences about self in subareas (e.g., English or math ability), to academic and nonacademic areas, and finally to general self-concept. Shavelson et al. (1976) and Marsh (1989) found few correlations between academic self-concept and nonacademic self-concept (physical appearance, peer relationships, etc.). Marsh et al. (1983) found that academic self-concept was positively correlated with academic ability and that nonacademic self-concept was not correlated with either individual or school-average measures of these variables. Therefore, academic performance may have little effect on self-concept in non-academic areas (Marsh 1989), but it may have a strong effect on self-concept in academic areas.

Shavelson and Bolus (1982 provide evidence of the hierarchical nature of self-concept and its correlation with academic performance from observations of a group of junior high school students. It was discovered that general self-concept correlated highest with academic self-concept, next with subject-matter specific self-concept (i.e., math self-concept), and lowest with grades. In addition, subject-matter self-concept is correlated higher with grades in that subject matter (e.g., math) than with grades in other subjects. For example, math academic self-concept is related to math grades and not history grades. Correlations between self-concept and indices of academic achievement, such as grades and test scores have been reported consistently (Hansford & Hattie 1982; Shavelson & Bolus1982 .

Further evidence suggesting that academic self-concept correlates with academic achievement is provided by Hoge et al. (1995) in a two-year longitudinal study. A similar study conducted by Byrne (1986) investigated the correlation between self-concept and academic achievement among 832 high school students and illustrated strong correlations between general self-concept and academic self-concept.

In the Byrne (1986) study, an investigation of the relationship between self-concept and achievement for 832 senior high school adolescent males and females was conducted. The study showed that the correlation from general self-concept to specific grades was low. The relationship between academic self-concept and grades was strong. Math self-concept correlated with math grades. English self-concept correlated with English grades. Findings also indicated that academic self-concept correlated more with school grades than with standardized achievement scores. School grades in mathematics and English were correlated with math and English self-concepts.

A more comprehensive study involved a meta-analysis of 128 studies conducted by Hansford and Hattie (1982) which provided evidence of the relationship between measures of academic self-concept and academic performance. Anglos in the

uncorrelated with other self-concepts such as nonacademic self-concept (Marsh et al. 1983; Shavelson & Bolus 1982. However, only a few studies have shown any significant evidence of the directionality or causal predominance of self-concept over achievement or vice versa.

Causal Predominance

These studies suggest that there is a relationship between academic self-concept and achievement but there is very little support to suggest which factors we should focus on. Do we focus on raising the achievement levels or the academic self-concept of students? Although empirical research has shown that there is a correlation between self-concept and academic achievement, the directionality of the effect is not clear—whether self-concept influences grades or whether grades influence self-concept. However, understanding this relationship will provide educators with the tools to help low performing students improve.

Calsyn and Kenny (1977) used cross-lagged panel analysis in an attempt to show causality. They found that correlations of achievement at the beginning of the study with self-concept at six months later are higher than the correlation of self-concept at the beginning of the study with achievement at six months later. Academic performance (GPA) was shown to be causally predominant over self-concept of ability. Calsyn and Kenny (1977) concluded that academic performance more often affects their self-concept of ability. This assessment of that ability leads to changes in self-concept, which in turn leads to changes in academic performance.

Angry Little Men: Hypermasculinity, Academic Disconnect, and Mentoring African American Males

Shavelson and Bolus (1982) also conducted cross-lagged studies. They measured self-concept and the grades of seventh- and eighth-grade students at two times, six months apart. They found evidence of the causal predominance of self-concept over achievement. In Byrne's (1986) cross-lagged study of ninth-through 12th-grade students using two data collections six months apart, causal predominance between self-concept and grades were not found in either direction. Given the mixed results of these studies, we cannot offer a firm conclusion about the causal ordering of self-concept and academic achievement.

In addition, "self-enhancement" and "skill development" pose further problems in our analysis of self-concept and achievement. These two important educational methods focus on different means of obtaining academic success. For example, in the skills development approach, learning results from the identification and structured teaching of specific skills needed for academic success; immediate positive reinforcement further strengthens the child's correct response. Self-enhancement development stresses positive self-concept as a necessary prerequisite for learning. Both approaches appear to be necessary in enhancing academic performance, but they challenge the belief about the influence or directionality of self-concept. For example, most researchers believe that changes in self-concept, if they occur at all, are a consequence of academic success rather than an intervening variable necessary for learning to occur. Studies associated with junior high school students and intervention programs did not show many strong differences between randomly selected and control groups (Scheirer & Kraut 1979).

Furthermore, the self-enhancement model states that perceived evaluations of others cause self-evaluation of one's ability, which in turn stimulates academic achievement. For example, in a nurturing school environment where one is encouraged and challenged to succeed, students will tend to self-evaluate ability and try to meet the expectations of others. Conversely, the skill development theorists argue that self-concept variables are primarily consequences of academic achievement or failure. While both theories (Scheirer & Kraut 1979) are used in intervention programs, the lack of empirical evidence showing the effect on long-term academic performance and self-concept suggest that more study needs to be done in this area.

Other studies cited by Scheirer and Kraut (1979) found that most interventions produced some effects on either self-concept or achievement but not both. In other words, educational interventions have not led to an association between self-concept change and academic achievement. The reasons for this are as follows:

- Methodological problems with the study design and types of data collected;
- Practical implementation problems such that the intended intervention was not actually taking place;
- Theoretical problems with the specification of the processes by which enhanced self-concept might influence academic achievement;
- An erroneous premise such that self-concept is not a viable mechanism for enhancing academic achievement.

Angry Little Men: Hypermasculinity, Academic Disconnect, and Mentoring African American Males

In all the theories reviewed in this study, self-concept is viewed as a variable necessarily intervening between various sources of self-concept formation and performance on academic achievement measures. An alternative view is that academic motivation comes from one's social environment. In this view, enhanced self-concept is an outcome of academic improvement *and* social approval.

Although causality is not evident in the literature, we do find significant evidence that self-concept is hierarchical and that there is a strong relationship between academic self-concept and academic performance. These results suggest that academic self-concept is a reflection of academic successes (James 1925). Therefore, we should expect low standards of achievement to be associated with low academic self-concept; high standards of achievement should be associated with high academic self-concept. The literature supports this theory, especially for Anglo students. However, we find some inconsistencies, as mentioned by Marsh (1989), with African American children.

This discrepancy between the academic self-concept of Anglo and African American students warrants further investigation, specifically of African American males and the weak correlations between their academic self-concept and performance (GPAs, standardized tests). As mentioned previously, current models, which were developed based on the observations of middle-income Anglo students, are not universally applicable. Clearly, there is a need for a model that incorporates cultural, socioeconomic, cognitive, and behavioral variables unique to African American male students.

Chapter 3: Academic Self-Concept of African American Males

Previous studies suggest that academic self-concept is related to academic performance such as grades and standardized achievement tests. However, studies involving African American students tend to be less reliable and lack the strength associated with academic performance. Although African American males usually show confidence in all the basic subjects, they tend to lack the evidence to support their beliefs. Thus, research involving academic self-concept and academic performance has faltered for this group of students.

In this chapter, we will identify and analyze how certain cultural factors may contribute to academic dysfunction in African American males. While some life experiences are not unique to African American males, they play a larger role in their everyday lives than found in the lives of typical Anglo students. Furthermore, these life experiences may shed light on the inadequacies of the instruments used to measure academic self-concept for all groups of students.

Why isn't low achievement related to academic self-concept in African American males? According to Paton et al. (1973), Anglo males may have more accurate academic self-concept in relationship to school achievement because of their life experiences. Environment, socioeconomic status, and outlook on life play a major role in academic success.

Research on African American adolescent males has generally focused on negative outcomes, such as incarceration, dropping out of high school, morbidity, and mortality. Deficit model studies prevent us from understanding the developmental processes of African American males. The *Portrait of Inequality 2012* suggests that African American children fall further behind as they progress through school (Children's Defense Fund 2012). As this report from Children's Defense Fund (CDF) outlines, in the fourth grade, 84 percent of African American public school students cannot read at grade level and 83 percent cannot do math at grade level. In the eighth grade, 86 percent of African American public school students cannot read at grade level and 87 percent cannot do math at grade level. Furthermore, African American students score the lowest of any racial/ethnic student group on the ACT (American College Testing Program) and SAT college entrance exams. African American males are not inherently inferior to other races or to females, yet they are not achieving at the same levels. Why?

The experiences of African American adolescents are complicated by many cultural and social factors generally not experienced by Anglo youth. According to Spencer et al. (1991), developmental concerns, such as identity and self-image, increased independence, relations with peers, school achievement, and career goals, are complicated by cultural, economic, and social forces that interact in complex ways (Spencer, Swanson, & Cunningham 1991).

In fact, in a number of social indicators such as poverty, unemployment, and crime, African American children and youth fared considerably worse than their Anglo counterparts over the past two decades, according to *Portrait of Inequality 2012*. As a result, they are disproportionately and adversely affected by social, demographic, and economic changes in American society (Hare

1985). For example, although infant mortality declined significantly during the past two decades for Americans in general, African American infants are still twice as likely to die as are Anglo infants (*Portrait of Inequality 2012*). In addition, African American males were the only group for whom the average life expectancy actually continues to be the shortest (National Center for Health Statistics 2011). African American males ages 15 to 24 are six times more likely than Anglo males to die from homicide. Compared to their Anglo counterparts, African American adolescents are far more likely to reside in low-income families (Children's Defense Fund 2011; The Urban Institute 2009). Whether they live in a one- or two-parent household, African American adolescents are more than twice as likely as Anglo youth to live below the poverty line (U.S. Bureau of Census 2010).

African American males are challenged by low education, unemployment, and high crime environments. Although the current educational trend shows improvement in dropout and high school graduation rates, African American males still have the poorest outcomes (Aud et al. 2012). For example, more African American youth are likely to drop out of school than Anglo teenagers. In 2010, the dropout rates for African American and Anglo youth residing in suburban areas were nearly equal (National Center for Educational Statistics 2010). Although the academic performance of African American students has notably improved, substantial gaps remain in school achievement (NCES 2010). African American adolescents tend to score below the national average on standardized tests and earn lower grades than students in the nation as a whole (Barton & Coley 2010), resulting in low educational attainment, unemployment, and high criminal activity.

Angry Little Men: Hypermasculinity, Academic Disconnect, and Mentoring African American Males

While African American males were approximately 16 percent of persons under age 18 in 2010, African American youth accounted for half (51 percent) of the arrests for violent crimes (murder, forcible rape, robbery, and aggravated assault), a quarter (25 percent) of all juvenile arrests for drug violations, and a quarter (24.5 percent) of property crimes (burglary, larceny-theft, motor vehicle theft, and arson) in that year (U.S. Department of Justice 2009). The overrepresentation of African American males among offenders has been attributed to a number of factors, including law enforcement bias in making arrests and bias in sentencing. High unemployment and poverty further exacerbate an already troubling situation.

African American males may be burdened by poverty and crime, but they still desire a better life, just like Anglo youth. The educational and occupational aspirations of African American youth equal that of Anglo youth (Rosenberg & Simmons 1973). Unfortunately, the evidence that quality of life can be enhanced is missing from their day-to-day experiences. In essence, unemployment remains high, businesses in the African American community are too few, and legitimate apprenticeship, mentoring, and work opportunities for African American adolescents are limited (Spencer, Cunningham, & Swanson 1991). Given these conditions, how can we help African American male students strengthen their self-concept and improve their academic performance?

If self-concept is a product of life experiences and an awareness of the judgments of others, stigmatized and oppressed groups should have a lower self-concept and self-esteem. However, this may not be the case.

Chapter 3: Academic Self-Concept of African American Males

A study conducted by House (1993) investigated 191 (124 African American and 67 Anglo) college students who were admitted to the university through a special admissions program for academically underprepared students. The students were first generation college students from low-income families. House measured academic self-concept, achievement-related expectancies, mathematics course grades, and composite scores on the ACT college entrance exam. The results showed that the math grades of students with low academic self-concept were significantly lower than those of students with high academic self-concept. Academic self-concept results showed no significant racial differences, even though differences were found in achievement levels on composite ACT scores. What this shows is that although African American students and Anglo students have similar academic self-belief, their actual performance on standardized tests were significantly different in favor of higher scores for Anglo students.

TABLE 1

Descriptive Statistics, Summarized by Student Gender and Ethnic Group

VARIABLE AND STUDENT GENDER	AFRICAN AMERICAN		ANGLO	
	M	SD	M	SD
Academic self-concept				
Male	10.05	1.59	10.12	1.49
Female	9.33	1.71	9.27	1.10
Mathematics grades				
Male	1.95	1.21	2.21	1.17
Female	2.18	1.04	2.52	1.18
ACT composite scores				
Male	13.26	3.36	16.00	3.05
Female	12.55	2.70	14.52	2.61

Angry Little Men: Hypermasculinity, Academic Disconnect, and Mentoring African American Males

As shown in the excerpt of Table 1 (House 1993), course grades in mathematics were very similar for both groups of students. Also, both sets of students had similar academic self-concept levels. However, African American males who had similar math grades and academic self-concept as Anglo males had ACT scores which were significantly lower. House suggests that a possible explanation is that African American males may have unrealistic expectations, or they may believe they are capable of achieving high goals but have not put together the tools to accomplish them.

Another study conducted by Gerardi (1990), evaluated 98 freshman engineering students at the City University of New York (CUNY). The sample consisted of 57 percent African American, 30 percent Hispanic, 5 percent Asian, and 4 percent Anglo. Each respondent completed the Brookover Self-Concept of Ability Scale (SCA) and the CUNY Freshman Skills Assessment Examination in reading, writing, and mathematics; composite GPAs were also factored into the analysis. The study found that the best predictor of GPA after three semesters in college for minority engineering students was initial academic self-concept. The findings in this study illustrate that academic self-concept is a good predictor of academic performance (GPA) at the college level. However, academic self-concept is far less useful a predictor of how well African American students will do on the ACT, SAT, and other placement tests.

Two studies (Jordan 1981; Mboya 1986) support the findings that academic self-concept is an important contributor to overall academic achievement for African American students. Mboya

(1986) studied the relationship among global self-concept, self-concept of academic ability, and academic achievement in 211 10th-grade African American students in five different public schools. The study measured the following items: global self-concept as measured by the Coopersmith Self-Esteem Inventory (SEI); self-concept of academic ability by the Brookover Self-Concept of Ability (General) Scale; and academic achievement by the California Achievement Test (CAT). The relationship between self-concept of academic ability and academic achievement was significant for grades. The relationship between self-concept of academic ability and academic achievement correlated more strongly than the relationship between global self-concept and academic achievement.

Jordan (1981) found similar results. Jordan investigated the contributions of global self-concept, academic self-concept, and need for academic competence to the variance in academic achievement of inner city, African American students. Data were collected from 328 (151 females and 177 males) eighth-grade students from low socioeconomic backgrounds. Global self-concept was measured via the Rosenberg's Self-Esteem Scale; Academic self-concept was measured by the Brookover Self-Concept of Ability Scale; the need for academic competence was measured by a questionnaire developed by Jordan (1979); and academic achievement was measured by composite GPAs for the academic year in the four academic subject areas. The relationship of academic self-concept to academic achievement (GPA) was stronger in females and males.

Additional findings (Busk et al. 1973; Paton et al. 1973) suggest that the self-concept of African American students does not differ from those of Anglo students. However, differences were found between the two groups when class rank and self-concept of ability were compared. Although the self-concept of ability scores were correlated with achievement tests, report card grades, and cumulative-grade average scores, the differences indicated that Anglo students had a more accurate self-concept of ability in relationship to their school achievement.

In most of these studies, African American students were from low-income families and segregated communities. Also, the studies typically analyzed the correlation between academic self-concept and school grades (GPA), which result in a strong relationship. However, when the studies evaluated the relationship between academic self-concept with standardized test scores, there was a very weak correlation. Given the increased utilization of standardized test scores to predict future educational outcomes, it is imperative that this relationship is reviewed further.

Hare (1980) compared 412 Anglo and 101 African American fifth-grade students to find whether children from varying backgrounds differ in their levels of academic self-concept. The measures used in this study consisted of a seven-item general self-esteem measure composed by Rosenberg. Self-concept of ability (SCA) was assessed by Brookover's five-item measure, and academic achievement was measured by performance on the math and reading sections of a standardized test administered district-wide. The findings showed that academic self-concept rose as socioeconomic status rose (with race controlled). When socioeconomic status was controlled, African American children scored significantly higher than Anglo children on academic self-concept; however, their performance on standardized tests was below that of their Anglo peers (see Table 2, excerpt; Hare 1980).

Table 2

Mean Scores on All Measures of Children

from Blue-Collar and White-Collar Families, by Race

(Hare 1980, excerpt of Table 3)

	GROUP							
	AFRICAN AMERICAN				ANGLO			
	Blue-Collar		White-Collar		Blue-Collar		White-Collar	
	(N=79)		(N=22)		(N=119)		(N=293)	
Measure	Mean	SD	Mean	SD	Mean	SD	Mean	SD
SCA	19.3	3.1	18.4	4.2	17.0	3.9	19	3.2
Reading	34.1	12.4	40.2	18.7	49.4	18.3	61.7	18.2
Math	33.1	12.4	34.3	16.4	45.3	19.8	56.8	21.4

Note. SCA stands for "self-concept of ability"

The results of this study are similar to the other findings reported in this section: academic self-concept is strongly related to the academic performance—school grades—for both African American and Anglo students. However, African American males' academic self-concept is distinctively less correlated than that of Anglo students. These findings may explain one possible limitation: the use of course grades as dependent measures. As pointed out by Wentzel (1991), course grades may reflect a number of student characteristics in addition to competence; attributes such as the effort and persistence required to complete homework assignments and exhibit classroom learning are different from the problem-solving skills required by standardized tests. Again, the lower performance by African American children on standardized tests provides several issues of concern as presented by Hare:

1. As others have suggested, African American children are unrealistic in their self-evaluations (Bachman & O'Malley 1986; House 1993; Marsh 1987).

2. African American children do not accept teacher and test evaluations as the sole criteria for estimating their ability.

3. African American children believe that someone or something is blocking their progress.

4. African American children use their social group as a benchmark to estimate their abilities.

Given these possible explanations, why would this unique aspect of self-concept exist for African American children?

Social Factors

As one evaluates the life experiences of African Americans it isn't difficult to understand how being a minority in America influences how people perceive them and how they may perceive themselves. Based on the stigmatized group's different experiences with poverty, mortality, and education, it is conceivable that their outcomes in life and perspectives on life may be different than those experienced by non-stigmatized groups. The experiences of stigmatized groups in America include economic adversity, social disadvantages, and political isolation. For example, African Americans of both sexes have fewer economic opportunities and lower economic outcomes in terms of earnings than Anglos (U.S. Department of Labor 2010). As documented earlier, African Americans are more likely to live in poverty, be affected by crime, and be exposed to less favorable social conditions than Anglos. African American students have lower academic achievement scores (Educational Testing Service 2011) than any other student group.

The negative outcomes in life, stereotypical low expectations, and discrimination should result in lower self-esteem and diminished self-concept. According to this perspective, members of stigmatized and oppressed groups who are aware that they are regarded negatively by others should incorporate those negative attitudes into the self-concept and consequently should have lower self-esteem (Crocker et al. 1991; Crocker & Major 1989). However, most literature suggests that stigmatized groups, especially African Americans, have levels of self-concept (Busk et al. 1973; House 1993; Jordan 1979;) and global self-esteem equal to or higher than that of Anglos (Porter & Washington 1979; Rosenberg 1979).

Some theoretical models (Crocker and Major 1989; Crocker et al. 1991) have examined stigmatized groups and tried to explain how certain stigmas and stereotypes may serve a self-protective function in minorities, especially in regards to academic achievement. The literature suggests that one's social group may actually serve as a buffer against negative comparisons. As a social group, it is common to avoid activities that put your social group at a disadvantage and to get involved with activities that highlight one's social group. When a group maintains certain activities to protect itself from ridicule or embarrassment it will discount these activities as not very important. These self-protective activities provide a theoretical foundation in helping reconcile the conflicting information regarding the weak relationship of academic achievement on standardized tests to academic self-concept within African American males. If African American males have high academic self-concept but low academic achievement on standardized tests, then what mechanism is buffering against low self-esteem? Although reports of unrealistic expectations (Hare 1980; House 1993) among African American students are commonly quoted, there are no direct theories presented to explain the possible discrepancies in the literature; however, several theories can be inferred from studies presented by Crocker and Major's (1989) findings in their research of stigmatized groups.

According to Crocker and Major (1989), individuals of stigmatized groups are vulnerable to being labeled as deviant, are targets of prejudice or victims of discrimination, or have negative economic and interpersonal outcomes. As a result of these unfavorable conditions of stigmatized groups, Crocker and Major (1989), as well as other theorists, believed that these conditions would be incorporated into the self-concept of the stigmatized. Thus, it is believed that African Americans may possibly elevate their academic self-concept to compensate for the negative perception associated with their poor academic performance. Rather than be embarrassed about their poor academic performance, they present a very positive belief system of their ability, despite the results. However, very few empirical studies support these findings. The researchers insist that members of stigmatized groups may buffer their self-perceptions in several ways, including:

1. Attributing negative feedback to racial prejudice;
2. Comparing themselves only to others in their own in-group rather than to the larger out-group;
3. Selectively devaluing those domains of performance on which their own group fares poorly and valuing those dimensions on which their own group excels.

Each of these self-protective mechanisms has some relevance for understanding African American boys' academic self-concept in relationship to low academic achievement on standardized tests.

Crocker (1991) studied whether negative feedback on a school assignment protects one's self-esteem by attributing the blame to others. Specifically, Crocker wondered if stigmatized groups protect their self-esteem by attributing negative feedback to prejudice. In the experiment, 38 African Americans and 45 Anglo students received feedback on a paper they wrote. The subjects were told they would be evaluated by an Anglo evaluator; some students could see him, and some could not. African Americans students were more likely to attribute negative feedback to prejudice than positive feedback. If the African American students could be seen, then they were more likely to attribute both negative and positive types of feedback to prejudice. This study provides insight into how African American students

Angry Little Men: Hypermasculinity, Academic Disconnect, and Mentoring African American Males

perceive the racial attitudes of their teachers and others, and those perceptions may or may not be accurate. Perceiving a teacher as prejudiced buffers African American students against low self-esteem, even if they performed poorly academically.

Crocker and Major (1989) suggested that several mechanisms are used to protect the self-esteem of stigmatized groups from the prejudices of others, including discounting the negative feedback and understanding that the prejudice of others has no relation to talents and abilities. Positive feedback, despite prejudice, was perceived as an accurate reading of ability. If African American students believe that others are being nice to them or evaluating their work positively out of sympathy for their condition or for fear of appearing prejudiced, then the positive outcomes do not enhance, and may even decrease, self-esteem (Crocker and Major 1989).

Crocker also studied whether the social group affects the self-esteem of low performing students. Social comparison theorists (Gibbons et al. 1994) say that we compare ourselves to others for feedback. Based on the feedback we receive, either we feel positive about the outcome and continue with habitual behaviors, or we feel negative and try to discount the feedback. If the feedback is too negative, one may select another group to compare with in order to obtain the feedback one desires. Some of the earlier studies (Hoffman et al. 1954) found that people will cease comparing with others whose performance level is clearly superior to their own. Clearly such comparisons are not very useful in terms of satisfying what is believed is the main goal of the social comparison process, which is self-evaluation (Gibbons et

36

al. 1994). On the other hand, comparison with others whose performance level is close to one's own can protect self-esteem.

Gibbons tested: 1) whether low performance of important tasks triggers self-protective strategies and 2) whether or not valuing academics actually enhanced self-perception.

Gibbons evaluated two studies: 1) a group of gifted students (13- and 14-year-olds) who participated in a three-week summer program and 2) a group of non-gifted college freshmen. Both groups had comparison preferences and self-perceptions assessed at the beginning of the experiment and then six months later. The students were asked to what extent and what (target group) level they engaged in social comparison, how often they engaged in temporal (past performance) comparisons, and how important academic and various nonacademic dimensions were to them. At the end of the session, they indicated how well they thought they had done in the program. The primary focus was on the students who thought they had not done well (Low Performance).

The researchers found that Low Performance boys lowered their preferred academic comparison level and raised their athletic comparison level. No other group showed a similar trend. It should also be noted that the initial analysis indicated that all subjects thought academics was more important than nonacademic activities. Self-concept, especially academic self-concept, of all students was very high at beginning and remained so six months later. The results did show that for gifted children, performance may affect the comparison group one targets and the importance of the task one places on failures or successes.

In the non-gifted sample of college freshmen (Low Performance subjects), they lowered their self-reported amount, lowered their level of academic social comparison, and lowered the importance of academics. They also raised the view of social status not related to academics such as popularity. The findings suggested that the decline in perceived academic importance among Low Performance students (primarily the boys in the adolescent sample) is consistent with the reasoning of a number of theorists who have suggested that importance of academics varies as a function of perceived competence (Harter 1986). Gibbons suggested that students appeared to be altering their comparison behavior to minimize being exposed to unfavorable comparative information. Lowering the amount of social comparison and the level at which it occurs both serve the self-protective function.

If we looked only at the similar abilities of African American students compared to Anglo students (based on standardized test scores), Marsh (1987) determined that children's academic self-concept is higher when they attend relatively low-ability schools than when they attend high-ability schools (Bachman & O'Malley 1986; Marsh & Parker 1984). These findings suggest that students in low-ability schools are probably less challenged intellectually but are able to feel better about their academic ability relative to the students against whom they compete. However, students at a highly demanding school with much stronger competition and higher performance expectations may have a lower academic self-concept relative to their peers even though their achievement levels may be higher. The big-fish-little-pond-effect asks if it is better to be more successful at a low-ability school or less successful at a high-ability school. It is believed that this relationship exists as a result of the in-group comparisons, where individuals evaluate themselves relative to others in their social environments. Additional findings suggest that stigmatized individuals are most likely to compare themselves with others who share a common fate.

African American students compare themselves with their in-group for the following reasons:

1. To mitigate the consequences of living in segregated environments (a proximity effect);
2. To obtain accurate self-evaluations (a similarity effect);
3. To avoid unpleasant or painful social comparisons (a self-protective effect).

Given the possibility of in-group comparison in the African American community, this is a likely explanation of the equal or higher academic self-concept relative to other groups. African American males may use only their same race peers or other poor performing males as a reference group, which is why it is possible to have high academic self-concept.

Another mechanism used by members of stigmatized or oppressed groups is to selectively devalue those dimensions on which they or their groups fare poorly and to selectively value those dimensions on which they or their groups excel. As noted earlier, it is acknowledged and accepted that African American students have lower achievement scores (Barton & Coley 2010) than any other student group. However, African Americans have contributed to other areas besides academics. The most notable contributions can be found in sports (track, football, baseball, basketball, etc.); African Americans have excelled in athletics over the past 50 years. Despite overcoming insurmountable odds (segregation, discrimination) in the sports industry and achieving wealth, African Americans as a whole still face the burdens of social and economic poverty.

Thus it is no wonder why most African American boys pursue sports rather than academic excellence in a quest for success. Gibbons et al. (1994) found that low performing boys lowered their preferred academic comparison level and raised their athletic comparison level in the face of academic failure. Young African American males believe being an athlete is a more appealing, attainable goal (given the models of success) than achieving in school. African American males have done their selected estimate of success in today's society associated with their social group and determined what is likely to provide success for them. They have evaluated the "rate of return" and decided that sports, not academics, will result in a big payday. Even though academics is socially desirable and most children want to at least appear smart, overindulgence and fantasizing about sports may protect African American males from the challenges they face with academics and failure.

For African American males, personal values are created, in part, by the patterns of positive and negative feedback that members of a group receive. According to the self-protective strategy used by some members of disadvantaged or stigmatized groups, overvaluing those attributes or domains in which their own group excels (i.e., sports) and devaluing those attributes at which the dominant group excels (i.e., academics), denies the power held by the dominant out-group. For example, it may be difficult to devalue achievement in a society that places great emphasis on individual success, but one can nevertheless place a greater value on domains in which one's own group appears to be advantaged.

Perhaps African American males compare themselves only to other African American males (in-group) when determining their academic competence. As such, the academic performance of Anglo children (out-group) may be irrelevant to the judgments African American males make about their own academic ability. Therefore, if an African American child uses only his same race peers as a reference group, it is possible to have high academic self-concept since he is no better or no worse in school than his in-group peers and still can have low academic achievement. This comparison is particularly true in relationship to the performance of Anglo males. In-group comparisons may serve as a protective function for the minority individual while blurring the relationship between achievement and academic self-concept. For example, when we use large samples collapsed across many different racial, ethnic, and social groups, quite often these conditions are confounded and it is not clear which, if any, is the critical variable. Though not addressed in the literature, the benefits of in-group comparisons may also provide encouragement and stability. It should be further noted that even within in-groups there are subgroups of individuals who may be achieving beyond that of the larger group; therefore, different self-protective mechanisms may be used by African American males who are excelling academically.

Supportive literature on African American males and their academic achievement (Poussaint & Atkinson 1970) suggests that given the high levels of global self-esteem and academic self-concept, the desire of African American males to achieve in school is high. Their parents have high expectations for their academic achievement (Rosenberg & Simmons 1973). However, the problem does not seem to be, as some have suggested, one of insufficiently high levels of aspiration, but rather one of realizing these aspirations through productive behaviors (Poussaint & Atkinson 1972). Other theorists (Katz 1968) suggest that African American socialization teaches the child the importance of scholastic achievement by laying down verbal rules and regulations about the classroom, coupled with punishment. But the socialization process apparently lacks guidance and encouragement of the child's academic mastery; therefore, the child learns only to verbalize standards of academic interest and attainment. Their standards then provide the cognitive basis for negative self-evaluations. The low achieving African American male learns to use expressions of interest and ambition as a verbal substitute for behaviors he is unable to enact. On the other hand, in Anglo socialization, academic achievement is taught by parents, teachers, and society as a whole.

Analysis

In summary, the literature has shown that academic self-concept is strongly related to most students' academic achievement. However, the research on African American males is limited and the findings are not clear. Academic self-concept is strongly related to students' grades (GPA) from school. However, when the academic self-concept is compared to results of standardized tests, the relationship is very weak for African American males relative to their Anglo counterpart.

The studies looked at African American children from low-income families and communities, which have many compounding issues (poverty, crime, inadequate resources, impoverished environments, single-parent households, etc.). The researchers neglected to sample children from middle- and upper-income African American families. These children tend to have more educational resources and are exposed to financial resources and goal setting activities. Sampling middle-income African American children might have revealed whether middle-class educational values and high expectations are conveyed to African American children and if that bears positively on academic self-concept and academic performance. African American children from middle-income families not only are repeatedly exposed to and come to value positive messages about education, they become equipped with the tools necessary to accomplish their academic goals.

Secondly, given the discrepancies found in the literature between African American and Anglo students, it is apparent that self-concept models are less than adequate in addressing the social context in which African American students develop academic skills (as measured by GPA, standardized test scores, and other objective standards of achievement). The models also failed to include family background, including parental occupation, income, and level of education. Models addressing family background could help identify a likely support group for African American male students. Whether formal or informal, the group can reinforce the message of "Yes you can!" It is also important to have access to mentors and teachers who can provide the guidance necessary to develop positive behaviors and beliefs that lead to success.

Most of the self-concept models failed to take into account antisocial behavior ("Do I get into trouble frequently at school?"). This might have provided insight into how children adapt to their academic environment.

Do African American males evaluate themselves with the same measures of success used by Anglo students? As mentioned, the academic self-concept of African American males is comparable or higher than that of Anglo students; however, as a whole, their performance on standardized tests is lower. These findings suggest that performance on standardized tests is not important to the academic self-concept of African American males. Apparently they believe they can succeed, but their behaviors do not lead to success.

The findings suggested that African American males may selectively devalue the academic arena while overly valuing sports. Given their limited exposure to successful academic role models and their overexposure to wealthy African American athletes via the media, it is no surprise which path they choose. Does the mere dream of a sports career compensate for their less than successful performance at school? It would be interesting if the literature addressed why the fantasy of a sports career outweighs the more achievable goal of graduating from college.

Do in-group peers serve as a mirror, a reflection, of the goals and aspirations of African American males? It appears that most poorly performing African American males assess their situation in the following manner: "If I'm doing so badly, I'm okay because I'm not alone." African American males compare themselves to their peers which may protect their self-reports because of the academically low comparison group. Whereas, most of the research on academic self-concept utilizes large samples from various communities, with varying demographics and school abilities, and combines the results. This combining of the results may not highlight the measurable differences you would find if your comparison group is academically weaker than the combined results. Furthermore, the studies do not address the in-group comparison, where low performing African American males tend to compare themselves to others who are also performing poorly in school. Given their low-ability school and their low-ability peers, it is no wonder that their academic self-concept is high.

The same can be said for high performing African American males; they compare themselves to high performing peers. Thus, it is not that African Americans have unrealistic expectations of their academic ability as others have alluded, but that their comparison group may be performing as poorly and receiving positive feedback. The positive feedback to the academically deficient schools with high performing African American males may be to encourage positive work due to their poor environment or low expectations. This may also raise the belief of some poor performing African American students that they are academically capable.

Without the ability to accurately assess the academic self-concept of African American male students, our teachers, parents, and mentors are ill equipped to help them achieve academically. Their future seems to be already written, unfortunately. Without a quality education or the self-concept to *realistically* assess their own performance, they will be doomed to poverty, unemployment, crime, and other social ills that jeopardize the American dream: the pursuit of liberty and justice for all.

Chapter 4: Hypermasculine Identity Development

Adolescence is a difficult time—identities are being formed, tested, and challenged by peers and family members alike. Adolescence becomes even more complicated when youth are surrounded by daily stressors and negative life outcomes (Cunningham 1999; Hare & Castenell 1985). In today's society, many youth face high-risk environments infested with crime, violence, poverty, and drugs. Research has shown that children who grow up in dangerous social environments are likely to experience future negative outcomes (Chestang 1972; Hare & Castenell 1985; Spencer 1995; Spencer et al. 1997). These negative life outcomes include lack of social responsiveness (violence), lack of financial resources (poverty), and poor career choices (unemployment). Although the predictive relation between risky environments and negative life outcomes has been well established, much less is known about the exact processes by which risky environments contribute to violence and poverty. One possibility is that impoverished environments lead children to develop attitudes and belief systems that constrain their future opportunities.

This chapter will investigate how potentially maladaptive attitudes and belief systems of adolescent students might relate to their level of engagement in the classroom. The maladaptive attitude that this research will investigate is Hypermasculinity. According to Mosher & Sirkin (1984), Hypermasculinity is the belief that danger is exciting, violence is manly, aggression is acceptable, and going against authority displays a sense of power.

Angry Little Men: Hypermasculinity, Academic Disconnect, and Mentoring African American Males

This overall belief system undermines school engagement because caring about and doing well in school does not fit into the hypermasculine persona. Furthermore, the at-risk context that promotes a hypermasculine disposition may also contribute to some of these same traits in female adolescents, thus potentially affecting their school engagement as well. Thus we will explore the relation between Hypermasculinity and school engagement for males. This chapter assesses whether males in stressful high-risk environments form a hypermasculine identity that is unique.

Identity Formation in High-Risk Youth

Research has shown that children who are raised in dangerous communities are at greater risk of dropping out of school, becoming involved with criminal activity, having inadequate job skills, and achieving fewer positive life outcomes (Cunningham 1999; Spencer 1995). Some children who live in high-risk environments seem determined to avoid being perceived as "teacher's pet," "brainiac," or simply as liking school (Ogbu 1986). This research investigated Hypermasculinity from a developmental perspective for children who live in environments with high levels of poverty, violence, and crime. From a social psychological perspective, Anderson (1999) theorized that some of these children believe they must choose between a life of decency or street life associated with "manliness" (Anderson 1999).

Although little research has addressed the developmental origins of Hypermasculinity, theory and personal observations suggest the following possible trajectory. Preschool aged boys growing up in low-income families may have parents who respond inconsistently to their behaviors, especially if they have difficult temperaments (Dishion et al. 1994). When these boys enter school, they may have difficulty complying with teachers' expectations and authority. At the same time, they may be exposed to older peers who provide examples of deviance, risk taking, and anti-authority behaviors. Furthermore, family members and peers expect boys to display toughness as a means of survival and gaining respect (Anderson 1999).

Hypermasculinity may emerge within the context of the school where peers interact, explore social rules of acceptance, and develop belief systems. As a result, young boys in school challenge each other with deviant behaviors, school apathy, and challenges to authority. A hypermasculine attitude may interfere with school performance because this identity includes resisting the compliant values of school, displaying a sense of school apathy, and discouraging others from participating in activities that conform to adult instruction. This hypermasculine identity forms the basis of responding to life situations with an abrasive and fearless attitude. Ultimately, Hypermasculinity leads to adverse life outcomes such as dropping out of school, deviant behavior, mental illness, poor health, and the inability to form healthy, intimate, stable relationships (Spencer 1995).

From a psychoanalytic view, Pleck (1981) proposes that Hypermasculinity results from difficulties males face in developing a positive masculine identity in the absence of a father.

He says that the mother-son relationship interferes with the development of positive masculine identity. As research has shown (Bowlby 1969/1999), children establish a strong attachment with the mother. For female children, this mother-daughter bond provides a positive context for feminine identity development. However, Pleck suggests that the mother-son bond leads to a feminine identity that has to be overcome through intense male identification.

Pleck proposes that male identification is created in relationship with the father, which leads to the rejection of feminine attributes. Male qualities and behaviors may include dominance, emotional control, participation in sports, and the display of toughness. However, in the absence of the father, boys are left to their own psychological devices, such as displaying an exaggerated masculinity or male bravado, what they think it means to be a man. This pretense includes fearlessness, toughness, and self-control (Mosher et al. 1984; Pleck 1981). Pleck (1981; Nettle & Pleck 1996) suggests that hypermasculine behavior is more prevalent in the African American community, where fatherlessness is a fact of life in more than 51 percent of households (Children's Defense Fund 2011; The Urban Institute 2009; U.S. Bureau of Census 2011).

Early Child Development

Compared to their Anglo counterparts, African American adolescents are far more likely to reside in low-income families (Children's Defense Fund 2011; The Urban Institute 2009). Whether they live in one- or two-parent households, African

Chapter 4: Hypermasculine Identity Development

American adolescents are more than twice as likely as Anglo youth to live below the poverty line (U.S. Bureau of Census 2008). African American adolescents tend to score below the national average on standardized tests and earn lower grades than students in the nation as a whole (Barton & Coley 2010), resulting in low educational attainment, unemployment, and high criminal activity. Although African American males make up roughly 6 percent of the population, they make up roughly 50 percent of prison inmates. Furthermore, the National Center for Health Statistics (2011) reported that African American males, ages 15 to 24, are six times more likely than Anglo males to die from homicide.

Educators and researchers continue to investigate solutions for reducing these alarming risks for African American males; however, few empirical studies have examined the early steps in this developmental trajectory. Few studies have provided an explanation of how male bravado or Hypermasculinity within the context of high-risk environments contributes to anti-social behaviors and school disengagement.

Hypermasculinity and Life Outcomes for Youth in High-Risk Settings

Several models have been proposed to explain adolescent identity development and its relationship to life outcomes (Brofenbrenner 1989; Gabarino 1982). Most of these models neglect the process by which risk contributors (poverty, violent communities, absent parents, academically challenged schools) affect individuals or how coping variables are associated with at-risk outcomes (Brofenbrenner 1989).

Angry Little Men: Hypermasculinity, Academic Disconnect, and Mentoring African American Males

The High Risk Model (Figure 1) that is proposed for this investigation includes how Hypermasculinity is affected by daily hassles, fatherlessness, school pressure, peer pressure, and maladaptive coping mechanisms.

The High Risk Model suggests that risk contributors affect the ability to cope with stress and daily hassles and utilize resources and parental support to meet the academic requirements of school. If the solutions addressing stress are positive, then a positive identity will be formed and school adjustment is obtained (Spencer 1995). However, if maladaptive solutions are utilized, Spencer (1995) and Cunningham (1999) have concluded that males may develop an overexaggerated male bravado disposition. Thus, males with this bravado orientation may develop hypermasculine attributes that will likely lead to school disengagement.

Figure 1. Hypermasculinity and School Engagement for

Youth in High-Risk Settings

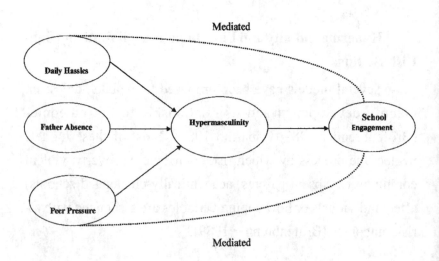

Chapter 4: Hypermasculine Identity Development

Empirical Support for the "High-Risk" Model

Evidence for the High-Risk Model is provided by two empirical studies that described in detail how daily stress and Hypermasculinity are related (Spencer 1995; Spencer et al. 1997). In the first study, Spencer (1995) presented data from the first year of a longitudinal study of African American male and female students, sixth through eighth grade, from a large city in the Southeastern U.S. Participants were part of a larger longitudinal study concerned with the development of competence and resilience in African American boys. Researchers investigated a hypothesized link between stress, engagement, and adaptive coping. Spencer (1995) suggested that danger and risk in low-income communities lead to a bravado orientation.

Participants completed surveys and interviews about daily hassles experienced, health-related behaviors, school and neighborhood context characteristics, particular life events, and social experiences. From the standard measures and interviews completed, four neighborhood-linked indices were identified:

- Violence and aggression experienced
- Risk experienced
- Perceived risk ("Do you perceive this as a risk? No/Never...Very/Always?")
- Perceived spiritual support ("Is religion important?")

Angry Little Men: Hypermasculinity, Academic Disconnect, and Mentoring African American Males

Students' bravado orientation, or Hypermasculinity, was measured using the machismo scale developed with college males (Mosher & Sirkin 1984). The machismo scale was derived from several iterations of questions (70 "calloused sex" items, 91 "violence as manly" items, and 60 "danger as exciting" items) that were narrowed down to 30 paired items that had the highest correlations for each subscale. The machismo scale consists of 30 paired items (one alternative in each pair) that described the callous, dangerous, or violent feelings of the participants. For each pair of statements, participants were asked which of the two alternatives would be truer for them; girls were asked to respond as they thought their male peers would.

The results from the study indicated that males reported more experiences of violence and aggression than females. For male participants, violence, aggression, and risk experience indices were significantly correlated with each subscale (danger, violence) of the machismo scale (Cunningham 1999; Spencer 1995). Furthermore, neighborhood factors of poverty, lack of resources, and violence were related to Hypermasculinity for the male participants. These findings support the research on anger and frustration conducted by Stevenson (1997) that noted that African American males, like most adolescents, integrate ideas about their identity from multiple sources, including the neighborhood environment (violence, danger, and poverty). Spencer's (1995) findings suggest male adolescents' machismo correlates with risk of violence and aggression.

Chapter 4: Hypermasculine Identity Development

Spencer et al. (1997) further examined the impact of risk on male self-esteem and learning attitudes. In this study, Spencer and her colleagues examined an achievement variable (negative learning attitude that represents an emergent identity) and hypothesized that an inverse relationship exists between general positive attitude (reactive coping method) and negative learning attitude (emergent identity) and that social predictor variable (stress engagement) would be associated with a negative learning attitude (emergent identity). Spencer concluded that the less social support students receive from teachers and peers, the more negative learning attitude they will exhibit as part of their emergent identity.

Participants in this study were African American students 14 to 16 years of age. They were examined utilizing components of high-risk identity development, such as an emergent identity (negative learning attitude) and its relationship to risk, stress, and reactive coping variables (social disaffection, social superiority, self-acceptance). This study assessed female family headship as a particular risk factor and two levels of stress engagement. Female headship was considered a risk factor due to the likelihood of the household living below poverty and residing in communities with high risk (National Center of Statistics 2011; The Urban Institute 2009). The two levels of stress engagement included stressful events in the past year and perceived social support (Spencer et al. 1997). Descriptions of stressful events in the past year (being stopped by police or victimized by violence) were obtained through interviews.

Furthermore, participants were assessed on perceived social support which includes popularity with peers and teachers. Perceived popularity was assessed based on the Self Sociometric Pupil Evaluation Inventory (SSPEI), which is a self-report measure designed to self-assess particular characteristics as perceived by others. General positive attitude was examined as a reactive coping method based on the Hare Self-Esteem Scale (1977). Negative learning attitude was derived from responses to the Perceived Positive/Negative Teacher Perception Scale (McDermott & Spencer 1995), which asked participants how the "typical teacher" perceived the student in areas such as attitude, disposition, and behavior. A high number of negative perceptions about the "typical teacher" classified the student as having a negative learning attitude. Likewise, a high number of positive perceptions about the "typical teacher" classified the student as having a positive learning attitude.

The researchers found that boys who have more stress have a positive learning attitude. For boys, being unpopular was linked to a less positive attitude and positively correlated with a negative learning attitude. These results provide compelling evidence that learning within high-risk, stressful environments does not necessarily lead to a negative learning attitude. Thus, children who may be overwhelmed with the challenges of life can still remain positive and have positive perceptions of their learning experience.

Despite the implications that stress in a high-risk environment affects the learning attitudes of school-aged children, there appears to be an inverse relationship between stress and negative learning attitude based on Spencer's results (1997). Furthermore, Spencer's study on neighborhood stress and negative learning attitude lacks a clear distinction between negative learning attitude (based on "typical teacher" perception) and the relationship to actual school performance (grades, school engagement). The learning attitude measure was developed to identify perceived teacher expectations of the student. The measure contains an equal number of positive and negative feelings relating to "how people feel toward and how people think of others, especially how teachers feel toward and think of children." For example, "My teacher thinks I am smart."

This study extended Spencer's findings by including a school engagement measure. Although this measure is self-reported, it provides a more objective look into behaviors that are associated with successful school performance (Finn 1993) than the "typical" teacher's perceptions. Thus, I contend that school engagement is a more valid construct and more likely related to important later outcomes.

Spencer (1995; et al. 1997) also studied stressors outside of school, for example, neighborhood violence, as well as learning attitudes and peer pressure. He found that neighborhood stressors are a strong predictor of inferred negative teacher perception and negative learning attitude. However, engagement in school and school performance were not examined as key contributors for academic success within these environments. Given the high incidence of Hypermasculinity (Cunningham 1999; Spencer 1995) and the evidence of poor school performance among this group, it is imperative to examine the relationship between these variables.

Chapter 5: School Engagement

African American males tend to be less active in responding to classroom questions and their participation in class engaging activity tends to be quite minimal. From classroom observations and self-report, they tend to be less enthused, less engaging, and show little interest in academic instruction because "it is boring". Furthermore, evidence indicates that they spend less time on homework and studying for a test. Research has shown that school engagement is critical to the learning and retention of academic subject matters. School engagement is described as active participation, completing assigned school work, paying attention to teachers' demands, arriving to class on time, and being involved in school activities (Finn 1993). School disengagement may be associated with truancy, dropping out of school, or even juvenile delinquency (Wehlage et al. 1989).

Finn found a developmental trajectory of school engagement that determines academic success or failure. School engagement in the primary grades may consist of a desire to attend, being prepared, and responding to the teacher's instructions or questions. As these students mature, they may take on a more active role of initiating questions and having a dialogue with the teacher. They may participate in activities during and after school or do more class work and homework than is required. Engaged students may assist other students or expand their participation to academic clubs and community activities. Finn says that engaged students set academic goals and critically think through their school performance.

Angry Little Men: Hypermasculinity, Academic Disconnect, and Mentoring African American Males

Measures of school engagement are significantly linked with students' success in the classroom, but this correlation is even more significant for minority students (Finn & Rock 1997; Spencer et al. 1997). Finn and Rock (1997) evaluated the effects of grade retention on school engagement and academic success with a large sample of minority students. In this study, African American and Hispanic students in grades eight through 12 were evaluated and classified as academically successful (did not repeat a grade or fail any classes) or poor academic performers (retained in one or more grades or failing school grades). Students in these categories were measured on self-esteem, locus of control, and school engagement (working hard, attending school, participating in class). Students' engagement in the classroom was measured by report card grades. The results suggested that significant school engagement was one aspect of academic success that distinguished students retained versus those passed on to the next grade. Self-esteem scores were not significantly related to school engagement. These results demonstrated that academic resilience is at least partially explained by the extent to which minority students are actively engaged in school. Overall, the results indicated that academically successful African American students are viewed by teachers as working harder in school, attending class regularly, getting in less trouble, and being more engaged in learning activities (Finn & Rock 1997).

In another study investigating school engagement of African American students, Connell (1994) found similar results showing academic performance significantly related to school engagement. The measures were based on the reports of teachers, parents, and students. Connell found school engagement to be significantly correlated with parental involvement. The students in this study were African American boys and girls ranging in grades five through 11. For this sample, parental involvement was linked to socioeconomic status. Poor families reported less engagement in school, thus showing that high-risk families produce more risky behavior and low school engagement. Furthermore, poor academic performance may be linked to a lack of parental support at home.

Brown et al. (1993) hypothesized that parenting practices were significantly associated with adolescent behaviors, which in turn were related to membership in adolescent crowds. He believed school engagement and achievement are heavily influenced by associations with peers and peer groups.

In this study, Brown administered surveys to 3,781 high school students (ages 15 to 19), parents, and friends to determine which factors most influence pro-social (school engagement and achievement) and anti-social (drugs) behaviors. Students were assigned on the basis of peer reports to various peer groups (brain, druggie, normal, jock, popular) and assessed on grades, peer group beliefs, parental styles, and parental involvement. Brown concluded that adolescent behavior (academic performance, drug use, and self-reliance) was mediated by parenting practices and crowd affiliation. For example, parents who used joint decision making with adolescents were more likely to have sons and daughters with higher grades who were less involved with the druggie crowd. Parenting practices positively affected adolescents' self-reliance and GPA. These results suggested that family, peers, and peer groups are major influences on adolescent school engagement.

Brown found that so-called jocks and normals have moderate academic achievement. Membership in the brains crowd was related to high grades and low drug use. On the contrary, membership in the druggies crowd was related to high drug use and low grades. Adolescents seem to have similar academic levels as their peer group mates. Thus, peers and peer groups may influence school engagement and achievement more than parents (Brown et al. 1993).

Hypermasculinity may develop when adolescents are confronted with in-group pressure to align with the general belief of the group. If they resist, their social rank may suffer. In some groups, such as popular, druggie, and jock, to maintain social rank, superiority, and toughness, adolescents may exhibit hypermasculine behaviors. If the ranking members of the group have disengaged from school, individual members may be swayed to feel the same way.

Fordham and Ogbu (1986) contended that for some African American youth, school disengagement may result when peer group and community norms persuade them that respect in the streets is the same as respect in school. Boys from at-risk communities perform below the standard set by teachers as a way to avoid perceptions of "acting white" or being seen as "brainiacs" or losing the respect acquired in the streets (Anderson 1999). Ogbu (1986) argued that the cultural-ecological perspective for examining this group must allow researchers to examine the school performance of minorities in the context of historical, structural, and cultural forces that tend to disregard the intellectual capacity of African Americans and glamorize their athletic contributions to society. Ogbu (1986) further suggested that deviant or pathological attitudes may reflect norms associated with their community. Thus, because other groups (European Americans) are assumed to have an advantage (financial or intellectual) in school, some cultures may discount academic achievement or school involvement as important or even possible for their peer group members.

Despite the positive relationship between school engagement and positive school outcomes, few studies have investigated the impact of African American academic disconnection. This academic disconnection may be a negative response to school achievement ("nerdy," "teacher's pet") or the subordinate behavior (students given demands by teachers but no respect) requested of adolescents who are challenged with the daily hassles of surviving in high-risk communities. From the perspective of some African American adolescents, a hypermasculine view of danger, respect, and power may contradict engaging in school, therefore reinforcing the academic disconnection.

Despite common community experiences influencing both males and females, academic disconnection may be more prevalent in males than females. Early socialization of gender roles and peer values around the school may be to blame. Young boys are taught to be self-reliant and independent (Pelligrini 1994). Males learn early on what type of independent behavior is valued by their peers in school and play. Given that noncompliant behaviors are often rewarded, this presents a problem in school (Pelligrini 1994). For example, males are rewarded for being rough, active, and popular with their peers, but when placed in the classroom they may regard the teacher's demands to sit still, wait in line, be quiet, etc., as too feminine (Pelligrini 1994). Thus evidence suggests that males as a group may be less engaged in school (Mosher et al. 1984). The belief that academics are for girls interferes with boys' academic goal-setting and classroom behavior (Pfeifer & Sedlacek 1974; Silverman & Dinitz 1974).

Maccoby and Jacklin (1974) suggested that boys and girls are rewarded differently in school. For example, boys are very competitive in the classroom and tend to engage in playful, boastful, and ego-challenging behaviors that interfere with meeting teachers' expectations (Maccoby & Jacklin 1974). Young girls tend to follow classroom rules and make better grades, perhaps in part because they are less involved with physically aggressive activities such as rough and tumble play.

Male socialization derives from societal expectations; boys in low-income communities are no exception. They are expected to be tough, in charge, and aggressive within the high-risk environment. Anderson (1999) suggests that male socialization in high-risk environments prompts them to observe and adopt behaviors (aggression) that will gain them respect, safety, and support. Thus, to conform to social expectations, boys behave in certain ways (Cunningham 1999; Spencer 1995).

Where do they learn these behaviors? Kids are very observant and school is definitely a teaching ground of good and bad behavior. Peers tend to teach the worst type of behavior and the most powerful and respected males in their communities are always looked upon as heroes to learn from. Unfortunately, these role models may not be upstanding citizens. At-risk boys quickly learn that nonchalance and aggression vs. school engagement are the keys to survival and respect in the community.

We often see class clowns, students with behavior problems, and students off task as essentially students who are disengaged. Some students attend school mainly for the social privileges and do not desire to learn, excel, or reach their full potential. They desire to be seen, noticed, feared, or respected; to cause laughter and gain respect from their peers. At the same time, they take away valuable learning opportunities and keep the teacher off task from teaching in order to maintain standards of classroom conduct. Students will continue down the same path because there are very few outcomes that prevent the student from being "disengaged" in the classroom. Often, the school system blames the teacher for classroom discipline but teachers are not encouraged to report this type of behavior because it isn't a "physically" disruptive offense. So, the teacher continues to try and teach and make minor adjustments to the situation. Eventually, the disruptive student continues to learn less and the other students struggle to understand why learning is important if this type of behavior can exist in the school. Thus, I wanted to study the relationship between hypermasculinity and school engagement.

Chapter 6: Investigation of Hypermasculinity and School Engagement

Mentoring is a very enlightening experience. After many years of engaging with at-risk young men I concluded that working with them outside of the classroom was beneficial to their experience with different activities and careers. However, most of the young men maintained their same level of academic competence, just passing. Few ever achieved the honor society, the principal's list, or the A/B honor roll. Mentoring was supposed to teach these young men to begin the journey to excel in all of their activities, including school. My goal was to help them be better students and although I was addressing their behavior when they were with me, I had no way to monitor or believe they conducted themselves so differently in the classroom. I recognized that their self-esteem and academic self-concepts were positive; however, their hypermasculinity prevented them from engaging in the classroom. Thus, I made it a part of the research for my master's thesis to investigate the relationship between Hypermasculinity and School Engagement among at-risk males.

This chapter reviews the study I performed and highlights the investigation of Hypermasculinity in African American male and female students in the sixth and 10th grades. I used female participants in the study for two reasons: to see if there were any significant differences in the levels between males and females and secondly, to see if the females were embracing the same mindset as their male peers. I wanted to find out if hypermasculine traits explain why some students do not become engaged in school. The measures included in this study assessed peer pressure, daily hassles, self-reports of school engagement, and father's support. School engagement variables assessed in this research included school attendance, grades, and class participation. Students' beliefs regarding various types of school engagement were also assessed.

I began my research with the following hypotheses:

1. Males from at-risk neighborhoods raised by a single parent show a higher level of Hypermasculinity than students from two-parent families. Studies have shown that Hypermasculinity is prevalent among African American males who come from single-parent families and high-risk communities (Cunningham 1999; Pleck 1981; Spencer et al. 1995). However, in these previous studies, a two-parent African American family comparison group was not included.

2. Males measure higher on the Hypermasculinity scale than females. Research (Mosher 1984) on college-age and adult populations has shown that Hypermasculinity is a characteristic of male participants and related to their view of aggression and violence. However, Mosher (1984) did not provide a comparison group of female participants. Furthermore, research suggests that males are more likely to exhibit overt aggression than females and more likely to view aggressive behavior as positive, whereas females view aggression as negative (Coie & Dodge 1998). Thus, we would expect males to score higher on hypermasculine behaviors and attitudes such as fighting, risk taking, and misogyny than females.

3. Older students score higher than younger students on Hypermasculinity. As older students become more socialized by their environments, the behaviors they believe are necessary to gain respect, cope, and maintain friendships become more prevalent and emerge within their own identities and belief systems (Spencer et al. 1997). Thus, our evaluation of students in the sixth and 10th grades may demonstrate a developmental increase in Hypermasculinity based on the learned experiences from their community, peers, and belief systems.

4. Males from high-risk communities report high levels of peer pressure (Peer Pressure Inventory). Research (Brown et al. 1993) suggests that students are influenced by the pro-social (school engagement and achievement) and antisocial (drug use) behaviors of peers. Peers may place pressure on their friends to conform to certain behaviors. Likewise, certain behaviors, such as Hypermasculinity, are used to identify with and receive approval from the group (Anderson 1999). Thus, boys who exhibit hypermasculine behaviors are more likely to measure higher on a peer pressure inventory and participate in groups who accept, portray, and maintain the hypermasculine behavior.

5. Hypermasculinity is correlated with low school engagement. In fact, Hypermasculinity and school engagement function as polar opposites. Research has found that Hypermasculinity is characterized by aggression, criminality, and substance abuse, whereas school engagement and performance are perceived as feminine. Similarly, research on school engagement has focused on specific behaviors in school and school outcomes but has neglected the impact of Hypermasculinity on academic

performance and engagement. If school engagement is a strong predictor of school performance (Connell et al. 1994; Finn & Rock 1997; Pierson & Connell 1992) and Hypermasculinity is associated with deviant school behavior (Mosher et al. 1984), then school disengagement is strongly related to a hypermasculine mindset.

Investigation Design

Participants in this study were male and female students in the sixth and 10th grades from a predominantly African American community within the North Texas area. Participants were asked to respond to several questionnaires: Life Experience Questionnaire (Cunningham, Spencer, & Swanson 1995), School Engagement Questionnaire (Finn 1993), Revised Hypermasculinity Inventory (Mosher et al. 1984), Peer Pressure Inventory (Brown et al. 1993), Family Information Survey, and Father Support Questionnaire. Children's Sex Role Inventory (Boldizar 1991), the Teacher Report Form of Child Behavior Checklist (Achenbach et al. 1991), and sociometric status measures (Coie and Kupersmidt 1983) were removed from this research due to the school district's demand to minimize the amount of classroom and home time the teachers and students spent on this research.

Investigation Participants

I had an opportunity to observe the schools and the participants several times before I started collecting data. The school district that I studied had a reputation for great sports teams. When I walked the halls and sat in the cafeterias I could tell the male athletes were definitely a part of the popular crowd. You could also tell there was a lot of bravado present. The kids were very hyped up about being active and being part of the social scene. They dressed in brand-name, colorful, stylish clothes. Students in the district's elementary and middle schools were less active and a little more reserved. At the high school level kids were all about the social rewards of being with opposite sex peers and engaging with friends. School was obviously a place for kids to engage with each other. The classroom was different—there was very little engagement, especially from the male students.

All male and female students in the sixth and 10th grades of one middle school and one high school were invited to participate in this investigation. Students were selected from low-income communities (based on census data) with a high population of African American youth. I encouraged participation by promising to reward a pizza party to the sixth- and 10th-grade classes with the highest number of signed and completed consent forms (whether children/parents agreed to participate or not). In addition, students who completed the questionnaires would receive extra credit in the class.

Although some of these measures were designed for boys (daily hassles and Hypermasculinity), questionnaires were constructed so that responses could assess whether hypermasculine characteristics, along with school disengagement, are evident in girls. Furthermore, including girls would allow further comparisons of male and female attitudes toward danger, violence, and school attitude.

Roughly 100 students participated (some students turned in their surveys partially completed). Participants ranged from 10 to 16 years of age. These children were old enough to perceive the daily hassles, socioeconomic risk factors in the community, and expectations for school success (Spencer 1995). The responses of younger students (10 and 12 years) could help me understand when Hypermasculinity is likely to emerge. Prior to the age of nine, children may not be able to understand the roles and images demanded by their communities, families, schools, and peers.

After approval was obtained from the school district and principals of each school, consent forms were sent to parents. I explained that through the study, I was seeking to understand how students' individual experiences (at school and with friends) contribute to school success. Parents were made aware of the confidentiality of their students' responses and the incentives (pizza party) for students who participate. I also explained the purpose of the study to the students and asked for their consent as well.

Investigation Procedure

The key to trying to obtain the most accurate responses from each student was to make this research appear to be something that will benefit all of us and not something merely for me. I tried to word the surveys and my introduction of them to emphasize that the answers were important but students should not struggle to answer any questions. There were no right or wrong answers.

Chapter 6: Investigation of Hypermasculinity and School Engagement

The younger kids were not very enthused about the different measures so I talked them through the experience and helped them see it wasn't that difficult. The high school students were somewhat excited because they looked at this as something different to do. They were excited about the extra credit and pizza party I offered.

Participants responded to six measures: Life Experience Questionnaire, Student Rating of School Engagement, Revised Hypermasculinity Inventory, Peer Pressure Inventory, Family Information Survey, and Father Support Questionnaire. Measures were administered in the classrooms of the students. Although some of the measures were specific to boys, the questions were centered on personal experiences so girls were asked to complete the same measures (with some rewording). I told the students that I wanted to understand their views about themselves, their schools, and their communities. There were no right or wrong answers, just their personal experiences. The administrator read the instructions for each measure as well as each item. This ensured that students were not influenced by their reading ability or fear of asking questions. The students completed each of the six questionnaires with their class or group and were then asked if there were any questions or concerns. When the project was completed, the students received a pizza party and the teachers were each given a $15 gift certificate.

Investigation Measures

Six measures were given to each student. In general, data were obtained from the most informed source for each measure whenever possible. For example, student classroom engagement levels were measured by self-reports.

Life Experience Questionnaire. The Life Experience Questionnaire is a revision of the Black Male Experience Measure (Cunningham, Spencer, & Swanson 1995). This measure examines the social experiences and daily hassles of students. Although the measure was appropriate for both males and females, it was revised in order to remove questions related to racial situations (e.g., "How often do White Americans generally think you are doing something wrong?") that I felt would not add any value to the investigation. The revised measure focuses on general feelings of daily hassles as opposed to hassles from any particular group. The measure examined perceived experiences of males and females by asking questions such as "How often do neighbors think you are doing something wrong?" and "When hanging out, do police or security stop and ask what you are doing?" Students were instructed to circle one of five responses for each question:

1. Never, if the event did not happen;
2. Almost never, if the event happened 1–3 times;
3. Sometimes, if the event happened 4-6 times;
4. Almost always, if the event happened 7–9 times;
5. Always, if the event happened 10 or more times during the last 12 months.

Student Ratings of School Engagement. The measures of school engagement were based on previous literature (Finn 1993) that analyzed students' basic compliance or noncompliance in the classroom. Seven total self-reported items from three individual points of view assessed school engagement. The first set of items assessed whether the student was absent or late to class and whether the student got into conflict with peers or teachers. The second set of questions measured being prepared for class and the students' engagement in school outside of the classroom as these factors related to the amount of homework assigned and completed. The third set of questions assessed the number of sports activities and academic extracurricular activities in which students participated.

Finn (1993) noted that the multivariate tests indicated that main effects for race, gender, and school performance were all statistically significant. Racial differences found that both Hispanic and African American students scored significantly below European American students on every achievement measure. Gender differences were attributable to the greater degree of non-cooperative behavior among males, whether reported by the teacher or by students themselves (Finn 1993).

Revised Hypermasculinity Inventory. The Revised Hypermasculinity Inventory is a revision of the Hypermasculinity Inventory (Mosher et al. 1984) which originally consisted of 30 questions with three subscales: danger, violence, and calloused sex. The Revised Hypermasculinity Inventory Measure was revised to accommodate the age of the participants. Questions regarding calloused sex and other inappropriate questions were removed, and some questions were reworded to accommodate the maturity level of the participants. The Revised Hypermasculinity Inventory included 10 items from the violence and danger subscales. Sample questions for danger included, "After I've gone through a really dangerous experience my knees feel weak and I shake all over," or "After I've been through a really dangerous experience I feel excited." A sample question for violence may ask, "It's natural for men to get into fights," or "Physical violence never solves an issue."

Several questions were added to include the perspective of girls and were written as the gender opposite of some of the male questions. For example, "Any woman who is a woman needs to have a boyfriend" was followed by, "Any woman who is a woman can do without a boyfriend." After each statement, the participant selected the statement that best fit her belief. The "violence as manly" subscale was a major contributor to aggression and dominance; in addition, that subscale had a small but significant positive correlation with defiance (Mosher et al. 1984).

Perceived peer pressure. The 75-item Peer Pressure Inventory (PPI) measured adolescents' perceptions of explicit peer pressure. Peer pressure was defined as, "When people your age urge you to do something or to keep you from doing something, no matter if you personally want to or not." The scale assessed peer involvement, peer conformity, school involvement, family involvement, and misconduct pressure. For example, questions ranged from "How strong is the pressure from your friends to: be social, do things with other people?" or "Go out for sports team?" Items for each scale were interspersed throughout the inventory. The four-point response scale indicated the degree and direction of pressure respondents felt from friends: "strong pressure," "some pressure," "a little pressure," or "no pressure."

Chapter 6: Investigation of Hypermasculinity and School Engagement

Family Information Questionnaire. This questionnaire was to elicit the following student information: age, sex, ethnicity, grade in school, caretaker (biological, adopted, etc.), and occupation of caretaker(s).

Father Support Questionnaire. This questionnaire was to elicit information about fathers or other significant adult males in the students' lives. Information obtained from this questionnaire will help us better understand the impact of fathers in students' lives. Pleck (1981) suggests that the absence of the father in the lives of young boys is critical to the development of hypermasculine behavior.

Findings

The results from the study are based on the statistical analysis performed on the data to see if the difference between age, gender, and grade were a factor. Also, the study analyzed whether any of the six measures had any significant relationships to each other.

My findings suggest that Hypermasculinity was prevalent among this group of students—and significantly more so among boys than girls. However, I did not find that boys living in single-parent households are more hypermasculine than boys in two-parent households. In fact, male students in two-parent homes measured higher on the violence and danger subscales of Hypermasculinity. I did not find any studies that looked into the impact of fathers (absent or present) on hypermasculine development in boys, and this is a serious omission in the literature. If we are to help African American boys succeed in school, we must begin to examine the role fathers play in hypermasculine development, especially in low-income, high-risk communities.

Research has shown that low-income fathers often lack emotional support and paternal engagement, and this may negatively influence their children's responses to adverse situations (Brooks-Gunn et al. 1999). For example, when pushed, boys often fight rather than exhibit self-control. Conflict resolution skills are sorely lacking in boys who display hypermasculine tendencies. Fathers exacerbate their boys' behavior by acting aggressively themselves. Through the father, a son may be introduced to a lifestyle of risky behaviors and out-of-control life challenges.

Studies have examined how the presence of the father is associated with male identity or male bravado. Pleck (1981) proposed that fatherlessness can lead to male bravado. Pleck further suggests that positive masculine identity is interrupted when boys are raised by a single mother. We would expect a higher measure of Hypermasculinity from single-parent homes, but this is not the case, as was mentioned before.

Furthermore, the findings that there are significant differences between one- and two-parent homes suggest that the presence of the father has a significant and positive impact on child development (Zimmerman, Salem, & Maton 1995), specifically on the social, emotional, and psychological development of the child (Biller et al. 1997; Cummings et al. 1997; Zimmerman et al. 1995). The impact of fathers on Hypermasculinity has not been studied; however, research has shown that the father's absence does not necessarily influence overall outcomes. The quality of the relationship is the greater influence of positive outcomes. Thus, for African American males, the positive role model, whether at home or not, influences positive outcomes. Research has shown that if the father is accessible, shows concern, engages with the child, provides proper discipline, helps with learning, and is a significant role model then the outcome is positive. Fathers who provide emotional support help model emotional security, which is reflected in the child's positive social, behavioral, and emotional responses.

The verbally and physically abusive behavior, negative communication, and hypermasculine behaviors and attitudes of fathers negatively influence boys. Consequently, the paternal role and belief system within at-risk communities are magnified when the father's behavior supports the hypermasculine culture. Fathers may expect their sons to display tough bravado behaviors in order to gain respect and survive (Anderson 1999).

As a result, my hypothesis that boys raised by single mothers are hypermasculine lacked evidence. However, the evidence did show that boys from two-parent homes often *are* hypermasculine. Clearly this is an important issue for future research.

My second hypothesis—males report more Hypermasculinity than their female peers—was found true as expected. Boys reported higher levels of Hypermasculinity than girls did for each subscale (violence, danger, and calloused sex). Males also report higher hypermasculine risky activities, including resisting authority and exhibiting adult behaviors (Spencer 1995). Also, males were more likely to view these behaviors as positive while females viewed them as negative (Cunningham 1999).

I found support for the third hypothesis: high school students measured significantly higher on the Hypermasculinity measures than middle school students. High school students reported a significantly higher level of violence than did middle school students. These findings support previous research that showed that over time, negative attitudes of African American males are learned and associated with negative contextual experiences (Cunningham 1999). Furthermore, Cunningham found that the developmental increase in Hypermasculinity levels may be a coping strategy for survival in high-risk environments. Adolescents are more aware of the negative things in their neighborhood (poor school, crime, liquor stores) as they get older, more so than younger children.

The research did not support the fourth hypothesis, that males experience high levels of peer pressure. Brown et al. (1993) defined peer pressure as the direct or indirect influence on the way one behaves, thinks, and accepts the norm. The mean reports on the peer inventory were not significantly different between gender or age groups. Perhaps most students in this sample felt similar levels of peer pressure or they had a similar definition of what influences them. Previous research showed that boys may be more influenced by their peers as a result of the high levels of risk taking and behavior issues related to negative outcomes (Cunningham 1999). Also, previous research suggests that African American males' perceptions of neighborhood characteristics are related to how adolescent males interpreted and integrated their social experiences, thus influencing the way they behave, think, and accept life outcomes (Cunningham et al. 1996). Cunningham (et al. 1996) suggests that adolescents turn to peers for social support and acceptance even when the outcome is negative and goes against what they believe to be the right thing to do. Despite our results that did not find a significant relationship between peer pressure and Hypermasculinity, it is likely that these students simply refused to acknowledge the impact of peer pressure on their behaviors. Hypermasculine males believe in their own independence and autonomy. If they acknowledged that peer pressure influences their behavior, that means they are followers, not leaders, and dependent on the beliefs and behaviors of others. They may not be able to discern or acknowledge the powerful ways peers exert pressure to act out negatively.

Furthermore, indirect peer pressure may be as much of an influence as direct peer pressure. Examples of indirect peer pressure include wanting to be liked by a particular group. At-risk boys may not see this as peer pressure but as a rite of passage through challenges and teasing.

It might be more fruitful to ask students how they see others responding to peer pressure. Boys are often reluctant to talk about themselves; however, they may be very willing to discuss others. We may be able to glean more information in this roundabout way than by asking direct questions. Indirect questions would tell us if students believe subtle comments have influenced the behaviors and beliefs of peers. Examples include:

"Does your friend hang with boys who are scared to fight?"

"If someone wanted to fight your friend, would he fight or walk away?"

"If your friend was a new student, how would he go about becoming accepted in your school or get respect?"

"Do students laugh at your friend when they answer questions in class?"

"Is it better to be able to fight or be smart in school?"

Different groups of students will respond differently to these questions. For example, at-risk boys accept the notion that "If someone talks about your mother, you have to fight him." If a student rejects this way of responding to a situation, then they might not be a part of the group, or they might even be picked on until they accept the male bravado orientation.

Recent literature has suggested that peer pressure has adversely affected African American students in the classroom (Fryer 2006). Fryer used the National Longitudinal Study of Adolescent Health, which studied 90,000 students from 175 schools in 80 communities who entered grades seven through 12 in 1994. Students responded to questions regarding friendship patterns, popularity, and academic success. African American males seemed to perform poorly in school in order to be accepted by their peers. Although students were doing poorly in school, there was no direct communication, no verbal instructions to fail. Fryer says the students accepted the fact that doing well in school makes you a nerd, and nerds aren't cool or accepted into various social groups. This population tends to ridicule students who are engaged in positive academic behavior. Thus, to do well in school is to be ridiculed, and to perform poorly is to be accepted. The popularity of all students decreased as their school grades increased, thus providing evidence that performing poorly in school may win you more friends and respect (Fryer 2006).

My fifth hypothesis, that Hypermasculinity is strongly related to school engagement, found no significant evidence or correlation between the Hypermasculinity subscale and the school engagement subscale. However, I did find that Hypermasculinity is prevalent in low performing schools; at least that was the case in the district I investigated.

Despite poor academic performance, at-risk students continue to have similar self-concepts as students with higher academic performance (Marsh 1989). I did not use a self-concept measurement in my study, but the idea is important. These students may report positive feelings about their academic performance (despite low GPAs) and their abilities because they relate their academic self with the other positive things that make up their overall school experience (popularity, friends, acceptance).

It is very likely that the self-report measurement tools used for this research did not provide adequate evidence because students lack objectivity and exaggerate their accomplishments and sense of engagement in school. Future research should include a teacher assessment of school engagement as a benchmark.

Our overall evaluation of these results suggests that student self-reports may have caused errors in our baseline data and thus our assessment. To better analyze these results, we must understand how male bravado or Hypermasculinity appears to teachers, parents, and other adults. In most cases, adults know that Hypermasculinity (toughness, individuality, independence) is a mask boys wear in at-risk communities. Typically, these boys are looked upon with great admiration by their peers when they display bravado, fearlessness, and anti-authority behaviors in and out of the classroom. Thus, I believe their academic self-concepts are maintained by their bravado and peer acceptance. Their academic rewards do not come from achieving high grades but from peer acceptance. These students maintain a positive self-concept of academic performance in the face of poor grades by maintaining the belief that they can do better if they tried harder. This makes them think they are smart enough to get good grades, but they have chosen to perform poorly within the classroom in order to win friends.

The results of my study should be interpreted in light of several methodological weaknesses. Some students had difficulty completing the multiple questionnaires. They made vague excuses as to why they didn't return the questionnaires. Some students complained that the questionnaires were too long and too complex to comprehend. Despite the teachers' efforts and incentives (extra credit and the pizza party), students were still unmotivated to complete and turn in the questionnaires. As a result of their lack of interest, it is likely that the results may contain errors due to their impatience and wanting to finish just so they could receive the reward.

The Hypermasculinity inventory used in this project may be more related to males' cultural view than students' actual self-identity. For example, males in low socioeconomic environments are more accepted if they endorse a hip-hop or "thug" look. This thug look may represent a desired cultural attitude but not necessarily the personal beliefs of the students (Anderson 1999). The thug look may be adopted just to win approval from their peers.

Another methodological weakness may be the self-report measure. It would have been ideal for self-reports to have been validated by teacher reports, parent reports, or report cards. Initially this research included three additional questionnaires that would have added some validity to the self-reports based on teacher reports and peer reports. The questionnaires were: the Child Sex Role Inventory, the Peer Sociometric Status, and the Teacher Report Form of the Child Behavior Checklist. The school district refused to release grades or teacher reports for the study. We do know that this particular school district has one of the lowest performing schools in the state of Texas (Texas Education Agency 2005). Based on observations and district academic reports, I believe academic engagement of male students is minimal, and this would have been revealed by cross-reports on behavior, academic preparedness, and state mandated tests (Texas Education Agency 2005).

An important methodological strength was that the sample was a minority group from a low-income community within a large metropolitan area. This provided an opportunity to study an underrepresented population. Few studies have examined how at-risk students feel about their fathers' support (or lack thereof). Much of the research suggests that fathers have a positive impact; however, few studies have evaluated the impact of fathers on academic success, especially for students in at-risk communities where Hypermasculinity is prevalent.

Future research should examine the link between Hypermasculinity and academic achievement. Standardized test scores would allow a more objective measure of students' academic performance rather than just classroom grades. Student grades in poor performing schools may not reflect the students' level with respect to other students at the school. In poor performing schools, students may make good grades and still have low scores on standardized tests. Since student self-reports may be unreliable, observations from parents, teachers, and counselors would be useful.

Further research on communication styles (with peers and authority figures) would help us understand problems related to peer pressure. We also need to know how peer groups are formed. How do students encourage others to engage in negative behaviors? By what criteria are students denied membership in peer groups? What makes some students popular and others not?

We must observe young boys at play, e.g., sports and video games. How is peer pressure displayed during play? How might peer pressure transform play, and even casual conversation, into Hypermasculinity and risky behaviors (cutting class, skipping school, getting into fights, not doing homework)?

Future research on at-risk boys must include a focus on Hypermasculinity. African American males make up roughly 6 percent of the population. However, nearly half of the prison population consists of African American males. We know that common at-risk contributors such as poverty, family structure, and violence are increasing at alarming rates: parents are divorcing at a rate of 50 percent, 51 percent of most African American children are raised by their mother alone, 39.1 percent children are in poverty, younger and younger children are entering the judicial system, and the academic performance of students in at-risk populations continues to be a concern (Cunningham 1999).

What has not been studied is the role of Hypermasculinity in this bleak scenario. Research is needed to determine how fathers in at-risk communities transmit hypermasculine behaviors to their sons. Given hypermasculine behaviors of aggression, anger, and rage, is child abuse prevalent? How do fathers transmit educational values to their sons? Are fathers involved in their sons' schools? How do fathers transmit ideas about discipline, responsibility, and accountability to their sons?

Future research should focus on accurately modeling the process by which youth form hypermasculine identities in disadvantaged communities and how Hypermasculinity influences life outcomes.

The Real World

We are often amazed at the loss of lives in at-risk communities. We see the symptoms but offer no solutions. Why do some boys in these circumstances succeed while others don't? This is what we need to discover. If there was a formula to create high achievers in the midst of educational apathy, then this book would not be needed. With more African American men in prison than in college, with the highest mortality rate of young men 15 to 24 years of age, and with an unacceptably high unemployment rate of almost 20 percent, clearly we are in a state of crisis.

It is past time to think and analyze how we can transform the lives of African American boys and men.

If there are at-risk students, there must be at-risk parents. If parents are at risk, then their families are at risk. If families are at risk then there are at-risk schools that reside in at-risk communities. If our communities are at risk then the cities are at risk. If our cities are at risk then the state is at risk. If the states are at risk, then America is at risk. So the question remains: How is it that we have so many at-risk males in America? And what does Hypermasculinity have to do with it?

This book has addressed the plight of young African American male students considered by most measures to be at-risk. We now understand that while their grades and test scores may be low, their academic self-concept is high. Their orientation is hypermasculine, but these behaviors and attitudes are counterproductive in the classroom. Hypermasculinity helps boys survive in the "'hood," but not in mainstream America.

Chapter 6: Investigation of Hypermasculinity and School Engagement

What we classify as academic at-risk is more than likely disengagement from school. When school becomes a boring, irrelevant place where no learning or effort happens, this is a recipe for disaster.

To help these boys, who have tremendous potential, we must begin to ask better questions and demand more cultural rigor of our research. Then we must implement what we learn in our homes, classrooms, and institutions. Mediocrity and failure are not acceptable.

Our challenge is to help our boys become excellent in everything they do. This book is a challenge to each mentor, teacher, parent, and community leader to start with the boys you know and work with them. Never give up, no matter their hypermasculine attitudes and behaviors. They need us, and we can't fail them. This is truly a life and death situation. Our very survival as a community is at stake.

In the next and final chapter, I will share with you my approach to mentoring African American boys.

Chapter 7: Angry Little Men

In this section I will present my personal insights from many years of mentoring, researching, and classroom experience. I believe the main reason why boys are behaving poorly in the classroom and failing academically is because of Hypermasculinity. This male bravado and emotion-driven responses, which are efforts to control their surroundings in the street, play a negative role in the classroom. When challenged in both the streets and the classroom their only answer seems to be along these angry paths. Young men who cannot control their anger or assess the situation before blowing up have an anger management problem. The remainder of this book will focus on positive ways to help young men cope with stressful situations and manage their anger.

Questions for Consideration

What's wrong? The challenges facing African American boys are colored by their environments and their perceptions of and reactions to others and life situations. These factors, compounded by community stressors such as poverty, violence, and a subculture that embraces toughness, reinforce negative behavior. In daily altercations with teachers, parents, peers, and even strangers, what starts off as a small issue is exaggerated into complex, self-destructing episodes of anger. The explosion appears to be the only way angry little men express themselves. Their inability to express an array of feelings, their self-doubt, fears, and uncertainty suppresses their awareness of a range of coping strategies while only increasing the anger within them. These boys don't seem to understand that what they are doing is wrong, unacceptable, and out of control.

Where is this anger taking place? Anytown, USA! No city is immune to angry boys who are out of control. Although the phenomenon is more prevalent in at-risk communities, angry little men can be found in any community that lacks role models who demonstrate self-control and self-respect. It is evident that something is wrong when you look at the suspension rate of African American males compared to all other students. African American students comprise 18 percent of the students in public school but 40 percent of all students who experienced corporal punishment.

Thanks to the pervasiveness of media, our boys are fed a daily diet of bravado, toughness, and thug behavior through hip-hop images. What are they learning from their media and community heroes and role models? Jay-Z, Little Wayne, 50 Cent, The Game, and so many other rappers serve as images of success to African American youth, communicating messages that often point toward bravado orientation as the route to success. What's more, during adolescence they're learning how to be a "man" and believe they are ready to call themselves men by showing their bravado. They demand their manhood rights from their parents, teachers, and peers without understanding or implementing nonviolent, comprehensive, culturally useful ways of first earning that noble title.

Chapter 7: Angry Little Men

How does interacting with peers via video games, texting, and emailing impact hypermasculine behavior? I believe the lack of real life, face-to-face interactions causes poor critical thinking skills and poor conflict resolution skills. Boys who lack the ability to properly communicate their frustrations, disappointments, or confusion will use their angry outbursts to save face and solve or escalate problems. Boys who get their messages from hip-hop images of power, toughness, bling bling jewelry, and fancy cars believe that you communicate by what you have and if that isn't enough, then you use force to settle your differences. The incidents may appear isolated, but these behaviors are taking place across America—in homes, schools, parks, and anywhere angry young men feel threatened physically, emotionally, or intellectually. Rage is the only expression that gets people's attention and demands power and respect.

When do we confront this behavior? There will always be resistance and blame for the behavior. Confronting this behavior is more difficult if you haven't spent time with these boys. As a mentor of at-risk youth, I know I will have to confront, discipline, or diffuse a situation at any time. I have experienced young boys on the same team go after each other after losing a game and blame each other. With no self-control they feel that they are disrespected and they can handle it only one way: through physical confrontation. That's why I spend a lot of time with them; it's the only way to gain their trust and respect. Each one needs to know that you care and that correction is a necessary part of caring. Investing time into the relationship will allow teachable moments to take place.

Angry Little Men: Hypermasculinity, Academic Disconnect, and Mentoring African American Males

How do we teach our angry little men to become good and respectful men committed to excellence? Boys are searching for so many truths: Who am I? What do I do with my life? Why don't they like me? Why is this so hard? The list goes on. When confronted with life's challenges, they blow up because they don't have any answers. I was once asked how I managed to get out of the pressure-filled, negative lifestyle of the streets. I thought about it and realized that I was intuitively making a C.O.D.E. switch. I had to adjust to a school mindset that I used in the classroom so I could learn how to thrive, and I had to go back to the street awareness mindset so I could deal with the obstacles confronting me in the streets.

C.O.D.E. switch probably saved my life and allowed me to excel in school and then maintain my self-image among my boys and others who watched me. I understood how to survive as a young African American man, displaying bravado, hanging with my boys, maintaining my respect among my peers. I was also an athlete and in those settings it was very important to display a tough exterior, similar to the streets. The classroom required a totally different set of skills: attention, discipline, hard work, school engagement, and kindness. Most of these traits I learned from my mother, some from teachers and friends. Mostly, I had to read my environment and determine what things I needed to do to survive in both worlds. Both were very important.

So, in order to help boys become more conscientious and respectful, we must have a plan in place to help them C.O.D.E. switch from being angry little men to healthy, academically successful boys to responsible, caring young men.

C.O.D.E. is an acronym I developed for mentoring boys. It stands for:

C = Connect to a VISION

O = Observation

D = Discipline

E = The Example

Developing the ability to C.O.D.E. switch from the tough attitude of the streets to more engaging behaviors in the classroom will help these young men find peace and a new direction to help them reach their goals. The following describes the C.O.D.E. approach.

C – Connect to a VISION

To learn any topic you must be engaged; the topic must be important and interesting to you. You have to connect to and make sense of the topic. In order to intrigue at-risk young men, you must minimize distractions so that they can connect to the VISION. Distractions are associated with background noise: street activities, peer pressure, and self-doubt.

What is the VISION? The vision you want to impress upon the minds of boys is about their future rather than their present state of mind. You must show them that they have a purpose in life and that their purpose *is* their vision. The vision is for them to become successful. Success may take the form of a mechanic, doctor, teacher, coach, engineer, lawyer, military officer, etc., but it all starts in the classroom.

How do you express this so that they will be motivated to do better? You must use their bravado and toughness to inspire them. Angry little men wear masks to protect themselves. Catchy, positive phrases that enforce their bravado are:

- Success is painful – *No excuses!*
- 1% Club – *No limits!*
- Just me – *Against the odds!*
- Man made – *On my own!*

The goal is to help them with their vision and then help them accomplish small successes in the classroom and at home. To connect with the vision is to get their attention and keep them hungry until you can feed them the whole vision. At-risk kids act like they have all the answers to life (and all the time in the world). They wear the hypermasculine mask so that no one can see that they are clueless and unsure of themselves, so do not be deceived by their bravado.

It is our job as mentors, teachers, and parents to recognize that our boys are well able to rise to the challenges of life without anger, violence, or other inappropriate, hypermasculine behaviors. They will quit trying if we allow hypermasculine behavior to control the situation. Young boys often get frustrated with school and begin to display a nonchalant or defensive attitude about classwork, homework, and improving their grades. They claim they have studied but they usually know very few people will help them. So we must change the attitude by sitting down and learning from them what they need by helping them with their work. No more excuses. If they make excuses, refuse to try, or perform below average, you must remind them that the world will give them nothing more than they give. Our angry little men are impressionable, so remind them that:

$E = mc^2$ (Albert Einstein)

...their Excellence (E) is determined by their Motivation (m) and Commitment (c) to succeed!

O – Observation

We first learned how to do things from observing our parents. We observed what they did, what they said, and how the world responded to them. Thus, home was our first school with traditional schooling soon to follow.

School has played an important role in teaching us what we need to know. However, hypermasculine boys don't observe, they react. The importance of observation is difficult to understand, especially for at-risk boys because observation requires interest in a subject or the anticipation that something surprising is about to happen. Thus, to sharpen boys' observation (and learning) skills, first introduce the idea of observing self. Helping boys learn how to observe themselves will show them how they have been reacting to problems in ways that may have prevented them from being heard or understood. Observing self will reveal how aggressive communication does not usually achieve the best results. Self-observation teaches us that we are responsible for our own behavior, and we are responsible for modifying that behavior. This is called "personal accountability" and is one of the most difficult things for hypermasculine boys to learn.

One example that comes to mind happened when I was teaching school. Every student had to stand in line, a straight line, before the class was released to go. One of my hypermasculine boys was not exactly in line; he stood a little off to the side. I asked him politely to get in line. I guess he was having a male bravado day because he claimed he was in line and wanted to know why I was bothering him. I tried to ignore him and asked again. He decided he was in the right and let this episode escalate, getting upset and disrupting the whole flow of the day for himself and the entire class. This was a simple request and an example of being defiant to show his power. Basically he showed his inability to handle a small task and remained in trouble on several other occasions until he recognized he was the only one acting this way.

In order to commit to excellence, boys must begin to understand how their words, moods, and behaviors are preventing them from achieving their academic goals.

Observing self is the foundation for understanding all kinds of personal behaviors, positive and negative. Show hypermasculine boys that they will achieve power when they have mastered their own thoughts, emotions, and behaviors through self-discipline. Have your boys discuss or write about the confrontations they have faced at home, with peers and enemies, and at school, and how they could have handled them differently. (When you were angry what did you do?) In many cases, boys learn about right and wrong *away* from home which suggests that schools represent important settings for them to grasp the elements of right and wrong. Writing about their experiences helps boys see how their thoughts and emotions lead to certain behaviors. It is important for them to learn ways to manage their anger and control their thoughts. The written form permits reflection. The goal is to get boys to slow down, observe their inner world, and identify best choices for action. As boys learn the keys to self-observation, they will learn how to learn, and a new world will open up.

Boys believe in the rightness of their misguided behaviors; the hypermasculine identity does not permit them to see these behaviors as negative, wrong, or disruptive. They simply feel justified in whatever they do.

Another way boys can learn is by observing how their actions impact others. This enables them to become more objective about right and wrong, productive and counterproductive. Our boys need to understand how their anger impacts other people. Role playing negative incidents is an excellent way for boys to learn—but only when they cool off. They'll be better able to see clearly what they should and shouldn't have done after they have calmed down. Let's teach our boys that there are always better ways to handle stressful situations. The goal is to teach them how to visualize positive responses and diffuse anger.

D – Discipline

I've never known a boy who didn't want to change his life for the better. Still, most at-risk males rarely feel the need to show restraint, to show obedience to authority, or to display self-control. Discipline is the key to making positive life changes, improving character flaws, and reducing behavioral problems. Discipline is the ability to obey a set of strict rules, *regardless of how you feel*, in order to improve something. Boys learn that discipline leads to positive outcomes. For example, in football, moving before the whistle signals the start is a violation; not passing the basketball to the open player is a selfish act. If you scream in class, you will go to the principal's office. If you discipline yourself and do your homework—*despite how you feel*—you will have a much better chance of getting a good grade than if you don't do the homework. Discipline teaches boys that there is a reaction for each action or a cause and effect relationship to most things, especially in school.

To respond to stressful situations with discipline requires an internal conversation. You have to remember what your goals are and if certain behaviors will, or will not, get you there. Saying things like, "This is how I am" or "I can't change" or "Why should I change" is a cop-out, not a disciplined response. The internal conversation must change to, "I can do better than this" or "Fighting will not help me achieve my goals."

The challenge is to get angry little men disciplined enough to change their thinking before something dramatic occurs. It's easier to see one's faults once inside juvenile detention, prison, or any bad situation that imposes isolation. We must help our angry little men to understand that either they become disciplined or succumb to needless struggle. To help boys get to this point is very difficult. Most of the time, they don't see why they need to change.

What will bring the angry little man to a point where he wants to change? A sense of urgency makes people do whatever it takes to correct or change their habits. Our boys are no different. If there is enough evidence that says you will live an unfulfilled life if you continue down this path, then you will become disciplined enough to change.

Chapter 7: Angry Little Men

We must help our boys see the coming storm on the radar screen; if it hits it could be devastating. For example, the three most challenging problems facing African American boys today are dropping out of school, going to jail, and dying. Boys who act out hypermasculine behaviors risk one or all of these negative outcomes. In the streets discipline isn't really required, you simply act out what you want and anger is an emotion that is accepted and applauded. However, in the classroom you need discipline to listen, to articulate your thoughts, to write down notes, to understand the examples, to evaluate, to think, and to make the right choices.

It takes discipline to take total responsibility for thoughts, words, attitudes, and behaviors, and we have to help our boys with this most difficult challenge. This is the only way their lives will turn around for the better. If in the past your student wasn't turning in homework, but he wants better grades, then every day he will need to do his homework, check his progress, and put some extra time in—be disciplined. If his behavior is a problem and the teacher constantly has to reprimand him, then he'll need to turn on the light and be less of a distraction—be disciplined. Your student will need to show up to school prepared to learn—disciplined and focused.

E – The Example

One way for boys to improve their lives is to seek out *positive* role models they respect and admire, and then observe and imitate them. Unfortunately, there are plenty of negative examples of Hypermasculinity to imitate in our communities and in the media, and that is why they believe that to intimidate is powerful, to resist authority is manly, and to become disengaged in school, because it may be boring, is acceptable. Their negative role models have taught them these things. Our little angry men think they can beat any obstacle and get away with anything because of who they are, but if they studied their negative role models closely, they would find many lives in ruin. They don't realize that by following these negative role models, the odds are now stacked against them. Unfortunately no one has made them understand the law of cause and effect. As a result, angry little men will try to beat the odds, but eventually they will have an unpleasant end (academic failure, prison, or death).

Our little angry men have not grasped the fact that to implement the C.O.D.E. for success, they must seek out and imitate the disciplined behaviors of good examples and positive role models.

Everything you can possibly want to do has probably already been done. Our good and bad habits are formed by observing others and actively learning. My best example is sports, especially baseball. Baseball is probably the easiest looking sport on television but the most difficult to perform in action. I have coached kids who could not hit the ball in practice or during a game. Until they grasped the example of how to hit the ball with their own consciousness and physical contact, they continued to wonder if it was even possible. Then the opportunity comes, the first hit ball meets bat, and they begin to learn. Through trials of success and disappointment, they begin to trust in themselves.

Chapter 7: Angry Little Men

The same process holds true for angry little men. One day a little angry man finds success in school or with a friend. Maybe he found the inner strength to walk away from a fight, resist peer pressure, or complete a homework assignment. Through his personal examples of positive interactions, positive communications, and positive self-assessment, he and other boys are on their way to becoming conscientious men. Our job is to help our little angry men recognize their own successes when they occur and then relate them to the new positive path they now walk.

The Mentor and Mentee Relationship

The best role model would be a parent or relative, someone a boy feels safe with and can trust. There are not enough fathers and men willing, present, or able to be positive male role models in African American communities, so we must find positive role models in other places. A good role model can be found in a mentoring group that has male mentors. There are various mentoring groups that provide this service for young at-risk males, but first, there are a few things to consider.

1. If you want to be a mentor, my best advice is to proceed with caution. Warning, warning, warning! Slow down, curve ahead, flashing lights! Being a mentor is a very important part of making a difference in the life of a young man. Despite the greatest intent to make that connection, it is rarely an easy thing to do. Despite your willingness to impart some valuable information to someone you feel could use it, it requires the other person to be receptive of this knowledge.

2. Often young men, especially angry ones, come to a mentoring program because they have been identified as someone who needs a mentor, someone who needs intervention, or someone who is going down the wrong path in life. Helping these young men can be a wonderful, though difficult, challenge that awaits the inspired mentor. Proceed with caution. Invest your time in getting to know the young man before you can suggest some changes. When he knows you care then he will take an interest in what you have to say.

3. Imparting knowledge requires two parties: one who has knowledge or information and one who needs to know. Until the young man decides he can trust you or that you really have something to offer, then he will be difficult to reach. His mind is often so far removed from adults that you will have to find some way to draw him into the purpose of the meeting. Why do the two of you want to meet? This is a learning experience for both of you. The mentor should want to learn something from mentoring as well.

4. As a mentor, your job is to share your experience and hopefully guide the young man down a path that brings pride to him, his family, and his community. To begin that process you must find a common area where you can begin to build trust. Sometimes we connect with boys by playing a game (checkers) or discussing sports (soccer or basketball). There may be interest in cars or your profession. It may take a little time before you figure out your mentee and begin planting seeds of positive change. Our goal is to plant the seeds and watch

them blossom. Even if a storm comes or the young man gets sidetracked, your involvement is important to the process of change. The goal is to give your young man some positive wins by helping him achieve success in the areas of concern. You probably will be his biggest cheerleader because it's likely he has never really been praised for doing well. Once he realizes that he can be successful in and out of school, he will slowly make the transition. It is a new way of thinking.

Being a mentor is about showing patience and believing that the young man will be all that he can be. We have to allow this transformation to happen, and that takes patience. The problems our boys face did not occur overnight. It will take time. Transforming the hypermasculine behaviors of our boys means we will have to be patient with the growing pains, be ready to support, and always be willing to smile in the face of disappointment. We are helping angry little men become familiar with the C.O.D.E. so they can gain success in school and life. Help our young men *Connect* to their vision for success, *Observe* their shortcomings so they can change, *Discipline* themselves to master self—thoughts, attitudes, and behaviors—and finally, seek positive *Examples* of success to follow. With this C.O.D.E., little angry men can begin to switch their mindset from the streets to the challenges in the classroom. We will begin to see academically successful young men growing up to be healthy and successful men. We will begin to see the beauty that had been hidden all along under the mask of Hypermasculinity.

Angry Little Men: Hypermasculinity, Academic Disconnect, and Mentoring African American Males

Appendix A: Tables from Research

Table 1: Mean Reports on Hypermasculinity Subscales by Age Group

	MIDDLE SCHOOL	HIGH SCHOOL
Danger	2.68 (1.58)	3.03 (1.49)
Violence	1.15_a (1.05)	1.61_b (1.14)
Calloused sex	.14 (.35)	11 (.31)

Note. Within subscale, means not sharing subscripts differed at p < .05.

Table 2: Mean Reports on Hypermasculinity Subscales by Gender and Parents' Marital Status

	VIOLENCE		DANGER		CALLOUSED SEX	
	Married	Not Married	Married	Not Married	Married	Not Married
Boys	1.85_a	1.19_b	3.61_c	2.68_d	.21	.22
Girls	1.11	1.30	2.56	2.59	.03	.04

Note. Within gender and subscale, means not sharing subscripts differed at p < .05.

Table 3: Mean Reports on Hypermasculinity Subscales by Gender and Fathers' Residence

	VIOLENCE		DANGER		CALLOUSED SEX	
	Y	N	Y	N	Y	N
Boys	1.70	1.27	3.68_a	2.48_b	.22	.21
Girls	1.18	1.27	2.61	2.56	.03	.04

Note. Within gender and subscale, means not sharing subscripts differed at p < .05.

Chapter 7: Angry Little Men

Table 4: Mean Reports on Peer Pressure Inventory Subscales

SUBSCALES	MIDDLE SCHOOL	HIGH SCHOOL
Pro-peer involvement	1.29 (.226)	1.41 (.276)
Pro-peer conformity	1.25 (.229)	1.25 (.237)
Pro-school involvement	1.12 (.169)	1.27 (.229)
Pro-family involvement	1.19 (.225)	1.25 (.244)
Pro-misconduct	1.15 (.181)	1.22 (.197)
Anti-school involvement	1.14 (.196)	1.21 (.214)
Anti-family involvement	1.17 (.228)	1.23 (.251)
Anti-misconduct pressure	1.16 (.207)	1.19 (.226)

Table 5: Correlations between Hypermasculinity Subscales and
School Engagement Variables

				SCHOOL ENGAGEMENT			
	Days Missed	Fights	In-School Suspension	Brings Supplies	Homework	Activities	Sports
Danger	.006	.149	.126	.206	-.147	-.041	.043
	.947	.077	.135	.014	.081	.631	.609
Violence	.005	.087	.149	.255	.072	.056	.003
	.950	.304	.076	.002	.393	.510	.967
Calloused sex	.072	.041	.120	.217	-.077	-.067	-.008
	.393	.628	.154	.009	.360	.429	.924

Table 6: Summary of Hierarchical Regression Analysis for Variables Predicting a
Subscale of Hypermasculinity, Violence (

VARIABLE	B	SE	Pr > |t|	β
Male	0.011	.232	0.964	0.005
Proximal Negative Experience	0.791	.186	0.0002	0.434*
Distal Negative Experience	-0.215	.155	0.172	-0.141
Pro-Misconduct	1.254	.746	0.097	0.214*
Anti-School Involvement	-0.490	.713	0.494	-0.091
Father Support	0.157	.103	0.131	0.149

Note: * indicates the model was statistically significant for variable p < .05

107

Angry Little Men: Hypermasculinity, Academic Disconnect, and Mentoring African American Males

Table 7: Summary of Hierarchical Regression Analysis for Variables Predicting a Subscale of Hypermasculinity, Danger

VARIABLE	B	SE	Pr > | t |	β
Male	0.586	0.353	0.100	0.174
Proximal Negative Experience	0.957	0.302	0.002	0.351*
Distal Negative Experience	-0.098	0.238	0.681	-0.043
Pro-Misconduct	-0.090	1.136	0.937	-0.010
Anti-School Involvement	1.094	1.086	0.317	0.135
Father Support	-0.080	0.156	0.608	-0.051

Note: * indicate the model was statistically significant for variable $p < .05$

Table 8: Summary of Hierarchical Regression Analysis for Variables Predicting a Subscale of Hypermasculinity, Calloused Sex

VARIABLE	B	SE	Pr > | t |	B
Male	0.190	0.066	0.005	0.298
Proximal Negative Experience	0.083	0.057	0.146	0.161*
Distal Negative Experience	-0.085	0.045	0.060	-0.196*
Pro-Misconduct	0.350	0.213	0.105	0.210
Anti-School Involvement	0.152	0.204	0.458	0.099
Father Support	-0.018	0.029	0.531	-0.0619

Note: * indicate the model was statistically significant for variable $p < .05$

Table 9: Summary of Hierarchical Regression Analysis for Variables Predicting a Subscale of School Engagement, Days Missed

VARIABLE	B	SE	Pr > | t |	β
Male	-0.177	0.149	0.239	-0.127
Proximal Negative Experience	0.358	0.128	0.006	0.316*
Distal Negative Experience	0.115	0.101	0.255	0.121
Pro-Misconduct	0.167	0.481	0.730	0.046
Anti-School Involvement	-0.797	0.460	0.087	-0.237*
Father Support	0.185	0.066	0.006	0.284*

Note: * indicate the model was statistically significant for variable $p < .05$

Chapter 7: Angry Little Men

Table 10: Summary of Hierarchical Regression Analysis for Variables Predicting a Subscale of School Engagement, In-School Suspension

VARIABLE	B	SE	Pr > | t |	β
Male	0.100	0.076	0.190	0.145
Proximal Negative Experience	0.016	0.065	0.808	0.028
Distal Negative Experience	0.030	0.051	0.553	0.064
Pro-Misconduct	0.536	0.244	0.031	0.298*
Anti-School Involvement	-0.018	0.233	0.940	-0.011
Father Support	0.035	0.034	0.295	0.110

Note: * indicate the model was statistically significant for variable p< .05

Table 11: Summary of Hierarchical Regression Analysis for Variables Predicting a Subscale of School Engagement, Days Missed

VARIABLE	B	SE	Pr > | t |	β
Male	-0.171	0.155	0.271	-0.123
Proximal Negative Experience	0.439	0.137	0.002	0.388*
Distal Negative Experience	0.049	0.100	0.627	0.052
Pro-Misconduct	0.521	0.484	0.285	0.143
Anti-School Involvement	-0.862	0.450	0.059	-0.257
Father Support	0.208	0.065	0.002	0.319
Violence	-0.192	0.074	0.012	-0.309
Danger	0.056	0.048	0.251	0.134
Calloused sex	-0.301	0.232	0.199	-0.138

Note: * indicate the model was statistically significant for variable p< .05

Table 12: Summary of Hierarchical Regression Analysis for Variables Predicting a Subscale of School Engagement, In-School Suspension

VARIABLE	B	SE	Pr > | t |	β
Male	0.049	0.080	0.544	0.071
Proximal Negative Experience	-0.025	0.071	0.724	-0.045
Distal Negative Experience	0.057	0.052	0.278	0.121
Pro-Misconduct	0.439	0.250	0.084	0.244*
Anti-School Involvement	-0.083	0.233	0.724	-0.050
Father Support	0.041	0.034	0.230	0.127
Violence	0.015	0.038	0.696	0.049
Danger	0.023	0.025	0.359	0.112
Calloused sex	0.230	0.120	0.060	0.212*

Note: * indicate the model was statistically significant for variable p< .05

Appendix B: School District Demographics

The school district demographics for research:

Population	21,045
Total children	5,562
Median household income	$31,153
Median home value	$46,600
Total households below poverty	18%
Total student population	2,902
Percentage of students African American	70.4
Percentage of students Hispanic	25.4
Percentage of students Anglo	3.9
Percentage of students that qualify for free lunch	60-70%
445th out of 481 districts	Students who took the SAT
Average score on the SAT	782 (462nd out of 465 districts)
Percentage of SAT takers who scored above 1100 in the class of 2002	0%

Bibliography

Achenbach, T. M., Howell, C., Quay, H. C, & Conners, C. K. (1991). National survey of problems and competencies among four- to sixteen-year-olds: Parents' reports for normative and clinical samples. *Monographs of the Society for Research in Child Development, 56*(3), 1–120.

Anderson, E. (1999). *Code of the street: Decency, violence, and the moral life of the inner city.* New York: W. W. Norton & Company.

Aud, S., Hussar, W., Johnson, F., Kena, G., & Roth, E. (2012). *The condition of education 2012.* Washington, DC: NCES, U.S. Department of Education.

Bachman, J. G., & O'Malley, P. M. (1986). Self-concepts, self-esteem, and educational experiences: The frog pond revisited (again). *Journal of Personality and Social Psychology, 50*(1), 35–46.

Baron, R., & Kenny, D. (1986). The moderator-mediator variable distinction in social psychological research: Conceptual, strategic, and statistical considerations. *Journal of Personality and Social Psychology, 51*(6), 1173–1182.

Barton, P. E., & Coley, R. J. (2010). *The Black-White achievement gap: When progress stopped.* Princeton, NJ: Educational Testing Service.

Bem, S. L. (1974). The measurement of psychological androgyny. *Journal of Consulting and Clinical Psychology, 42*(2), 155–162.

Bledsoe, J. (1967). Self-concept of children and their intelligence, achievement, interests and anxiety. *Childhood Education, 43,* 436–438.

Boldizar, J. P. (1991). Assessing sex typing and androgyny in children: The children's sex role inventory. *Developmental Psychology, 27,* 505–515.

Bowlby, J. (1969/1999). *Attachment.* Attachment and loss (vol. 1). (2nd ed.). New York: Basic Books.

Bronfenbrenner, U. (1989). Ecological systems theory. In R. Vasta (Ed.), *Annals of child development* (pp. 185–246). Greenwich, CT: JAI Press.

Brookover, W. B., Thomas, S., & Paterson, A. (1962). *Self-concept of ability and school achievement* (Final Report of

Cooperative Research Project No. 845). East Lansing, MI:
Educational Publishing Services.

Brookover, W. B., Thomas, S., & Paterson, A. (1964). Self-concept
of ability and school achievement. *Sociology of Education,
37*, 271–278.

Brown, B. B., Mounts, N., Lamborn, S. D., & Steinberg, L. (1993).
Parenting practices and peer group affiliation in adolescence.
Child Development, 64(2), 467–482.

Brown, S. (1979). The health needs of adolescents. In *Healthy
People: The Surgeon General's report on mental health
promotion and disease prevention* (DHEW, PHS Publication
79–55071A). Washington, DC: U.S. Public Health Service.

Busk, P., Ford, R., & Schulman, J. (1973). Effects of school's
racial composition on the self-concept of Black and White
students. *Journal of Educational Research, 67*(2), 57–63.

Byrne, B. M. (1984). The general/academic self-concept
nomological network: A review of construct validation
research. *Review of Educational Research, 54*(3), 427–456.

Byrne, B. M. (1986). Self-concept/academic achievement
relations: An investigation of dimensionality, stability, and
causality. *Canadian Journal of Behavioral Science, 18*(2),
173–186.

Calsyn, R. J., & Kenny, D. A. (1977). Self-concept of ability and
perceived evaluation of others: Cause or effect of academic
achievement? *Journal of Educational Psychology, 69*(2),
136–145.

Chestang, L. W. (1972). *Character development in a hostile
environment* (Occasional Paper No. 3, Series, pp. 1-12).
Chicago: University of Chicago Press.

Children's Defense Fund (2011). Black and White: Black children
compared to White children. Washington, DC: Author.
Retrieved from Children's Defense Fund website: http://
www.childrensdefense.org/child-research-data.../black-and-
white-black.pdf.

Children's Defense Fund (2012). *Portrait of inequality: Black
children in America.* Washington, DC: Author. Retrieved
from Children's Defense Fund website: http://
www.childrensdefense.org/child-research-data-
publications/data/portrait-of-inequality-2012.pdf.

Coie, J. D., & Dodge, K. A. (1998). Aggression and antisocial
behavior. In W. Damon & N. Eisenberg (Eds.), *Handbook
of child psychology* (pp. 779–862). New York: Wiley.

Bibliography

Coie, J. D., & Kupersmidt, J. B. (1983). A behavioral analysis of emerging social status in boys' group. *Child Development, 54,* 1400–1416.

Connell, J. P., Spencer, M. B., & Aber, J. L. (1994). Educational risk and resilience in African-American youth: Context, self, action, and outcomes in school. *Child Development, 65,* 493–506.

Cooley, C. H. (1902). *Human nature and the social order.* New York: Charles Scribner's Sons.

Cooley, C. H. (1956). *Two major works: Social organization. Human nature and the social order.* Glencoe, IL: Free Press.

Crocker, J., & Major, B. (1989). Social stigma and self-esteem: The self-protective properties of stigma. *Psychological Review, 96*(4), 608–630.

Crocker, J., Voelkl, K., Testa, M., & Major, B. (1991). Social stigma: The affective consequences of attributional ambiguity. *Journal of Personality and Social Psychology, 60*(2), 218–228.

Cunningham, M. (1993). Sex role influence on African American adolescent males: A literature review. *Journal of African American Male Studies, 1,* 30–37.

Cunningham, M. (1999). African American males' perceptions of their community resources and constraints: A longitudinal analysis. *Journal of Community Psychology, 27,* 569–588.

Cunningham, M., & Spencer, M. B. (1996). The Black male experiences measures. In R. L. Jones (Ed.), *Handbook of tests and measurements for Black populations* (pp. 1–6). Hampton, VA: Cobb and Henry Publishers.

Deaux, K., & Major, B. (1987). Putting gender into context: An interactive model of gender-related behavior. *Psychological Review, 94,* 369–389.

Dishion, T. J., Patterson, G. R., Stoolmiller, M., & Skinner, M. L. (1991). Family, school, and behavioral antecedents of early adolescent involvement with antisocial peers. *Developmental Psychology, 27*(1), 172–180.

Educational Testing Service (1985). *The reading report card.* National Assessment of Educational Progress. Princeton, NJ: National Center for Educational Statistics.

Epps, E. G. (1969). Correlates of academic achievement among northern and southern urban Negro students. *Journal of Social Issues, 25*(3), 55–70.

Finn, J. D. (1993). *School engagement and students at risk.* Washington, DC: National Center for Education Statistics.

Finn, J. D., & Rock, D. A. (1997). Academic success among students at risk for school failure. *Journal of Applied Psychology, 82*(2), 221–234.

Fordham, S., & Ogbu, J. (1986). Black students' school success: Coping with the "burden of 'acting White.'" *Urban Review, 18,* 176-206.

Garbarino, J. (1982). *Children and families in the social environment.* New York: Aldine.

Gerardi, S. (1990). Academic self-concept as a predictor of academic success among minority and low socioeconomic status students. *Journal of College Student Development, 31,* 402–407.

Gibbons, F. X., Benbow, C. P., & Gerrard, M. (1994). From top dog to bottom half: Social comparison strategies in response to poor performance. *Journal of Personality and Social Psychology, 67*(4), 638–652.

Hansford, B. C., & Hattie, J. A. (1982). The relationship between self and achievement/performance measures. *Review of Educational Research, 52*(1), 123–142.

Hare, B. R. (1977). Racial and socioeconomic variations in preadolescent area-specific and general self-esteem. *International Journal of Intercultural Relations, 1*(3), 31–51.

Hare, B. R. (1980). Self-perception and academic achievement: Variations in a desegregated setting. *American Journal of Psychiatry,* 137(6), 683–689.

Hare, B. R. (1985). Reexamining the achievement central tendency: Sex differences within race and race differences within sex. In H. P. McAdoo, & J. L. McAdoo (Eds.), *Black Children.* Beverly Hills, CA: Sage Publications.

Hare, B. R., & Castenell, L. A. (1985). No place to run, no place to hide: Comparative status and future prospects of Black boys. In M. B. Spencer, G. K. Brookins, and W. R. Allen (Eds.), *Beginnings: The social and affective development of Black children.* Hillsdale, NJ: Lawrence Erlbaum Associates.

Bibliography

Harter, S. (1983). Developmental perspectives on the self-system. In P. H. Mussen (Ed.), *Handbook of Child Psychology: Socialization, Personality, and Social Development, 4,* 275–385.

Harter, S. (1986). Developmental perspective of the self-system. In E. M. Hetherington (Ed.), *Handbook of child psychology.* New York: John Wiley & Sons.

Hoffman, P. J., Festinger, L., & Lawrence, D. H. (1954). Tendencies toward group comparability in competitive bargaining. *Human Relations, 7,* 141–159.

Hoge, D. R., Smit, E. K., & Crist, J. T. (1995). Reciprocal effects of self-concept and academic achievement in sixth and seventh grade. *Journal of Youth and Adolescence, 24*(3), 295–314.

House, J. D. (1993). Achievement-related expectancies, academic self-concept, and mathematics performance of academically underprepared adolescent students. *The Journal of Genetic Psychology, 154*(1), 61–71.

James, W. (1892). *Psychology: The briefer course.* New York: Holt, Reinhart, & Winston.

James, W. (1902/1925). *The philosophy of William James.* New York: Modern Library.

Jordan, T. (1981). Self-concepts, motivation, and academic achievement of Black adolescents. *Journal of Educational Psychology, 73*(4), 509–517.

Katz, I. (1968). Academic motivation and equal educational opportunity. *Harvard Educational Review, 38,* 56–65.

Lasane, T. P., Howard, W. L., Czopp, A. M., Sweigard, P. N., Bennett, G. G., & Carvajal, F. (1999). Hypermasculinity and academic goal setting: An exploratory study. *Psychological Reports, 85,* 487–496.

Maccoby, E. E., & Jacklin, C. N. (1974). *The psychology of sex differences.* Stanford, CA: Stanford University Press.

Markus, H., & Nurius, P. (1986). Possible selves. *American Psychologist, 41,* 954–969.

Marsh, H. W. (1987). The big-fish-little-pond-effect on academic self-concept. *Journal of Educational Psychology, 79,* 280–295.

Marsh, H. W. (1989). Age and sex effects in multiple dimensions of self-concept: Preadolescence to early adulthood. *Journal of Educational Psychology, 82*(3), 417–430.

Marsh, H. W. (1990). The structure of academic self-concept: The Marsh/Shavelson model. *Journal of Educational Psychology, 82*(4), 623–636.

Marsh, H. W. (1991). The failure of high ability high schools to deliver academic benefits: The importance of academic self-concept and educational aspirations. *American Educational Research Journal, 28*(2), 445–480.

Marsh, H. W. (1993). Academic self-concept: Theory, measurement, and research. In J. Suls (Ed.), *Psychological perspectives on the self,* vol. 4 (pp. 59-98). Hillsdale, NJ: Lawrence Erlbaum Associates.

Marsh, H. W., Parker, J. W., Smith, I. D., Barnes, J., & Butler, S. (1983). Preadolescent self-concept: Its relation to self-concept as inferred by teachers and to academic ability. *British Journal of Educational Psychology, 53*(1), 60–78.

Marsh, H. W., & Parker, J. W. (1984). Determinants of self-concept: Is it better to be a relatively large fish in a small pond even if you don't swim as well. *Journal of Personality and Social Psychology, 47*(1), 213–231.

Marsh, H. W., & Shavelson, R. J. (1985). Self-concept: Its multifaceted, hierarchical structure. *Educational Psychologist, 20*(3), 107–123.

Mboya, M. (1986). Black adolescents: A descriptive study of their self-concepts and academic achievement. *Adolescence, 21*(83), 689–696.

McDermott, P. A., & Spencer, M. B. (1995). *Measurement properties of revised scale of teacher expectations of Black males* (Interim Research Report No. 26). Philadelphia: University of Pennsylvania, Center of Health, Achievement, Neighborhood, Growth, and Ethnic Studies.

Mead, G. (1934). *Mind, self, and society.* Chicago: University of Chicago Press.

Mosher, D. L., & Sirkin, M. (1984). Measuring a macho personality constellation. *Journal of Research in Personality, 18,* 150–164.

Bibliography

National Commission on Children. (1991). *Beyond rhetoric: A new American agenda for children and families: Summary.* Washington, DC: Author.

National Center for Health Statistics. (2011). *Vital statistics of the United States, 2011.* Hyattsville, MD: Author.

Nettle, S. M., & Pleck, J. H. (1996). Risk, resilience, and development: The multiple ecologies of Black adolescents in the United States. In R. J. Haggerty, L. R. Sherrod et al. (Eds.), *Stress, risk, and resilience in children and adolescents: Processes, mechanisms, and interventions* (pp. 147-181). New York: Cambridge University Press.

Newman, R. S. (1984). Children's achievement and self-evaluations in mathematics: A longitudinal study. *Journal of Educational Psychology, 76,* 857–873.

O'Hare, P. O., Pollard, K., Mann, T., & Kent, M. (1991). African-Americans in the 1990's. *Population Bulletins, 46.* Washington, DC: Population Reference Bureau.

Ogbu, J. (1986). A cultural ecology of competence among inner-city Blacks. In M. B. Spencer, G. K. Brookins, & W. R. Allen (Eds.), *Beginnings: Social and affective development* (pp. 45–66). Hillsdale, NJ: Lawrence Erlbaum Associates.

Paton, S., Walberg, H., & Yeh, E. (1973). Ethnicity, environmental control, and academic self-concept in Chicago. *American Educational Research Journal, 10*(1), 85–99.

Pelligrini, A. D. (1994). The rough-and-tumble play of adolescent boys of differing sociometric status. *International Journal of Behavioral Development, 17*(3), 525–540.

Pfeifer, C. M., & Sedlacek, W. E. (1974). Predicting Black student grades with nonintellectual measures. *Journal of Negro Education, 43,* 67–77.

Pierson, L. H., & Connell, J. P. (1992). Effect of grade retention on the self-system processes, school engagement, and academic performance. *Journal of Educational Psychology, 84*(3), 300–307.

Pleck, J. (1981). *The myth of masculinity.* Cambridge, MA: MIT Press.

Poussaint, A., & Atkinson, C. (1970). Black youth and motivation. *Black Scholar, 1*(5), 43–51.

Porter, J. R., & Washington, R. E. (1979). Black identity and self-esteem: A review of studies of Black self-concept, 1968-1978. In A. Inkeles, J. Coleman, & R.H. Turner (Eds.), *Annual Review of Sociology, 5,* 53–74.

Rosenberg, M., & Simmons, R. G. (1973). *Black and White self-esteem: The urban school child.* Washington, DC: American Sociological Association.

Rosenberg, M. (1979). *Conceiving the self.* New York: Basic Books.

Ross, A. O. (1992). *The sense of self: Research and theory.* New York: Springer.

Scheirer, M. A., and Kraut, R. (1979). Increasing educational achievement via self-concept change. *Review of Educational Research, 49*(1), 131–150.

Shavelson, R. J., & Bolus, R. (1982). Self-concept: The interplay of theory and methods. *Journal of Educational Psychology, 74*(1), 3–17.

Shavelson, R. J., Hubner, J. J., & Stanton, G. C. (1976). Self-concept: Validation of construct interpretations. *Review of Educational Research, 46*(3), 407–441.

Silverman, I. J., & Dinitz, S. (1974). Compulsive masculinity and delinquency: An empirical investigation. *Criminology, 11*(4), 498–515.

Spencer, M. B. (1995). Old issues and new theorizing about African American youth: A phenomenological variant of ecological systems theory. In R. L. Taylor (Ed.), *African-American youth: Their social and economic status in the United States* (pp. 37–70). Westport, CT: Praeger.

Spencer, M. B. (1999). Social and cultural influences on school adjustments: The application of an identity-focused cultural ecological perspective. *Educational Psychology, 34,* 43–57.

Spencer, M. B., Cunningham, M., & Swanson, D. P. (1995). Identity as coping: adolescent African-American males' adaptive responses to high-risk environments. In H. W. Harris, H. C. Blue, & E. E. H. Griffith (Eds.), *Racial and ethnic identity* (pp. 31–52). New York: Routledge.

Spencer, M. B., Dupree, D., & Hartman, T. (1997). A phenomenological variant of ecological systems theory (PVEST): A self-organization perspective in context. *Development and Psychopathology, 9*(4), 817–834.